# THE CHANGE MAKERS

# THE CHANGE MAKERS

## MAKERS

Their influence on British business and industry

Cary L Cooper
and
Peter Hingley

**Harper & Row, Publishers**
London

Cambridge
Hagerstown
Philadelphia
New York

San Francisco
Mexico City
São Paulo
Sydney

British Library Cataloguing in Publication Data

Cooper, Cary L.
    The change makers: their influence on British business and industry.
    1. Success in business
    I. Title      II. Hingley, Peter
    650.1      HF5836

ISBN 0-06-318318-8

Typeset and printed and bound by
Butler & Tanner Ltd, Frome and London

# ACKNOWLEDGEMENTS

To all those who agreed to talk to us.

To Rachel and Laura, Scott and Beth.

To Jane.

To our determined secretary, Lesley, who has been involved in this book at every stage.

To Sheena Mackay for her help.

To Dick Ottaway for his initial support and encouragement.

# CONTENTS

# INTRODUCTION

# THE JUNGLE FIGHTER:
# A MYTH?

'I think I can recognise a real entrepreneur at 300 yards on a misty day! Like an actor he is full of self-confidence and vanity. But he trusts his vanity and feels that what he has to say really matters. He is interested in the prizes, in the money, and has got a way of looking at things which can make them add up to his advantage. He feels alone and knows that what he says matters, so being able to make and carry through his own decisions is crucial to him. Above all he has this drive to succeed and get things done. He needs to get up at 3 o'clock in the morning as he knows he is on his own and no one else is going to do it for him.'

This is Sir Peter Parker, former Chairman of British Rail and currently Chairman of Rockware, Mitsubishi Electric (UK) and the British Institute of Management, explaining his views on 'what makes them tick at the top'.

Sir Peter Parker was one of a group of 'change makers' interviewed as part of a project to identify characteristics that had led to their success. Our original group, numbering thirty-two, were identified by a panel of senior editorial staff of national newspapers. Individuals were chosen because they had made or were continuing to make a lasting change in attitudes within their own particular sphere of activity. Representatives were drawn from politics, industry, business, the arts, medicine and social work. As the interviews took place, we saw emerging a number of

1

fascinating characteristics that were shared by the group from industry, business and the unions. We decided to examine in more detail the common elements that lay behind the success of these individuals. We decided to expand the original sample in order to widen and to make more balanced the range of activities represented, and we selected a number of additions on the basis of their successful managerial achievements.

Not everyone from our original list or from our expanded list agreed to be interviewed. Those that did agree and were interviewed in depth were:

Sir Michael Edwardes, former Chairman of British Leyland and of International Computers and currently Chairman of Chloride and Dunlop Holdings

Lord Gormley, former President of the National Union of Mineworkers

John Harvey-Jones, Chairman of Imperial Chemical Industries

Jeremy Isaacs, Chief Executive of Channel 4 TV

Richard Ingrams, Editor of *Private Eye*

Clive Jenkins, General Secretary of the Association of Scientific, Technical and Managerial Staff

Prue Leith, Managing Director of Prudence Leith Enterprises and Board Director of British Rail

Lord Longford, former Leader of the House of Lords and Director of Sidgwick & Jackson

Elizabeth MacDonald, Marketing Director of Knight, Frank & Rutley

Jonathan Miller, TV and Theatrical Director and Producer

The Honourable Sara Morrison, a Director of General Electric Company

Clare Mulholland, Deputy Director of Television, Independent Broadcasting Authority

Len Murray, former General Secretary of the Trades Union Congress

Sir Peter Parker, former Chairman of British Rail and current Chairman of Rockware, Mitsubishi Electric (UK) and British Institute of Management

Mary Quant (and her husband Alexander Plunkett-Greene) of Mary Quant Group

2

Arthur Scargill, President of the National Union of Mineworkers
Lord Weinstock, Managing Director and Chief Executive of
General Electric Company

It has been suggested over the years, both in the popular press
and by management academics, that men and women who achieve
success in industry, business or in public life generally are strongly
motivated by an insatiable lust for power, and that their lives are
organized and meticulously designed to achieve the 'next rung on
the success ladder'. Michael Maccoby in his book *The Gamesman*
characterizes the successful American executive as all-consumed
with 'winning', detached from relationships, aggressive, and ice cold
under pressure. In other words, 'the game character is happiest
when his work is most like (competitive) play'. Alistair Mant in
his book *The Rise and Fall of the British Manager* highlights the
'survival type' of successful executive, 'so badgered by a sense of internal emptiness, that he cannot stop running (what makes Sammy
run is what is lacking from the start). He may not be a genius,
but his manic energies will ensure he "outsurvives" everybody.'

Successful entrepreneurs, executives and industrial leaders of all
sorts are characterized in popular fiction in the same ominous
tones. Joseph Heller did this in his excellent fictional account of
corporate life *Something Happened*. 'In the office in which I work
there are five people of whom I am afraid. Each of these five
people is afraid of four people (excluding overlaps), for a total of
twenty, and each of these twenty people is afraid of six people,
making a total of one hundred and twenty people who are feared
by at least one person. Each of these one hundred and twenty people
is afraid of the other one hundred and nineteen, and all of these one
hundred and forty five people are afraid of twelve men at the top
who helped found and build the company and now own and direct it.'

But is this reality? Are men and women who achieve executive
success really the demagogues and the power hungry climbers we
expect them to be or are they a breed apart, the self actualisers in
Maslow's *Toward a Psychology of Being*? 'Self actualising people,
those who have come to a high level of motivation, health and
self-fulfilment, have so much to teach us that sometimes they seem
almost like a different breed of human beings.'

In this book we raise and begin to answer some of these questions.

# CHAPTER ONE

# CHILDHOOD
# EXPERIENCES

*'The childhood shows the man, as morning shows the day.'*
John Milton

In considering how an individual functions we must make an attempt to take into account the important formative influence of life's experiences. Psychologists have always tended to look with close attention at the early years, hoping to reveal the origins of later attitudes, behaviour, success and failure. Although it has become something of a cliché to attribute adult problems to adverse childhood experiences, we believe, nevertheless, that we can see some definite links between the past and present in the group of 'change makers' we studied.

## INSECURITY AND LOSS

The young child, whilst not perhaps Locke's *tabula rasa* completely moulded by events, is nevertheless, dependent upon and at the mercy of his immediate environment. Significant experiences during these early years seem to have deep and lasting effects upon his/her subsequent personality development. Believing, like Carlyle, that 'The history of a man's childhood is the description of his parents and his environment', we delved into the early childhood experiences of our group. We were surprised to find that many thought of their childhood as being, in some way, a period of loss or deprivation. Many of them felt rootless, disorientated and lonely. But they also felt that they had emerged in some way different from their peers, having a certain 'strength through survival'.

For a number of those we interviewed the loss was grievous, the early death of a parent, or brothers and sisters during the War—an event that proved personally devastating. Lord Weinstock, Managing Director and Chief Executive of General Electric Company, whilst at pains to stress the ordinary nature of his own background, lacked the parental influence present in a normal family. As a child he had what he termed 'an orphanic existence'.

'My parents came to this country, at the beginning of the century, from Poland. They were refugees from Czarist oppression. My father was a master tailor and they lived in a working class environment in North London.

'Both my parents died when I was very young and I lived for a time with a brother. Then I was evacuated as a child with the other members of the state school which I attended and went to a school in Stoke Newington. It was a secondary school and it was supposed to teach commercial things. It did actually teach me bookkeeping. Simple double-entry bookkeeping. That stood me in very good stead, better than accounting really! That was a very valuable thing to have learned at an early age!'

He did not see the loss of family life as being especially traumatic, rather it was something he had simply not experienced: 'Don't forget, my parents had been dead for some years. I had five brothers, but they were much older than I was ... My next oldest brother lives in Canada, and he is 18 years older than I am ... So it wasn't that sort of family. My brothers were all married. They all had children of their own. So yes, I suppose I was in an orphanic position.'

Arthur Scargill, President of the National Union of Mineworkers, was totally distraught at the death of his mother: 'On a personal basis, the thing I think that hurt me more than anything else, and affected my life and disturbed me for a period of time,

was the death of my mother. When my mother died she was 50—
I was 18. I'm an only child, and the impact of that loss was
incalculable. I cannot describe adequately my feelings of utter
desolation. My whole life was literally destroyed overnight. The
life that I had, the atmosphere in my home, disappeared overnight.
The one regret that I have—every time I achieve something for
the public or whatever—it is I think of my mother ... and I feel
sad she isn't here to see it. That was a real personal blow of
immeasurable magnitude, as far as I was concerned.'

Len Murray, former General Secretary of the Trades Union
Congress, also experienced this 'orphanic existence', suffering a
succession of tragic losses. His early memories are of poverty and
degradation. Overshadowing it all was the cruel loss of both parents before he reached the age of nine.

He spoke with some feeling as he recalled the impact of those
early years: 'My father was a farm worker and my mother was a
farmer's daughter. We lived in Central Shropshire on the tip of
the Black Country, Wellington. So there were pits all around, and
steelworks and one or two factories. We were on the edge of town
and country. But I felt more of a rural than urban man.

'I was born in 1922, the year of the Great Strike. We were poor.
Well I remember Monday mornings at school—queuing outside
the headmaster's study for free tickets for dinners, while the rest
of the kids got theirs in the classes. This was searing! I felt very
bitter.

'Both parents died when I was very young and both had died
in accidents. My father died in an accident with some farming
machinery. Before I was nine my mother died, she was killed in a
bus accident, and then I went to live with an auntie, and then I
went to live with an uncle who had a small farm, on the edge of
poverty himself. You couldn't make a decent living out of farming
in those days. And then when I went to grammar school, I went
back to live with my auntie. So I became a bit isolated, solitary.
My main interest was books. I became an omnivorous reader—
any book I could lay my hands on.

'I had a hard fight to survive in school, and I'll say this for my
auntie, that she was absolutely intent on me getting an education.
If she hadn't been there I'd have left school. The idea was I'd stay

on my uncle's farm and so on and work there. She was very influential in developing my education—"Get upstairs and do your homework," she'd say, during the holidays! Hard, but fighting for it. Then she died just before I went to university the first time, and then that was it. There was no place to go.'

## SEPARATION FROM PARENTS

Several people also found themselves separated from their parents, usually by war or some other circumstance. A typical experience is that of Richard Ingrams, Editor of *Private Eye*. He was evacuated from London as a child of four: 'My childhood was really during the War. My parents originally lived in London and we were evacuated to Scotland for the whole of the war years. So I spent most of my early childhood in Scotland in my grandmother's house.

'I didn't see much of my father as he was working in London throughout the War and he died when I was 14. In fact, I did not get to know him all that well. So I was brought up in this "matriarchal" society consisting of my mother and grandmother.'

For some, the experience of separation stayed with them throughout their adult years. Jeremy Isaacs, Chief Executive of Channel 4 TV, was separated from his parents at the start of the Second World War, and this experience seemed to stay with him throughout his life. 'There was a traumatic jolt in our relationship, each of our relationships with our parents when the Second World War started, because on the 2nd September 1939 we were all sent out of Glasgow, in good care, but what turned out to literally be a traumatic period of separation from our parents. We were strangers in the part of the country that we went to, and I think that the strangeness of being an evacuee in the very pleasant surroundings of Kirkcudbrightshire and Galloway in south-west Scotland, coupled with the strangeness of being Jewish in rural Scotland, meant that (I certainly) always felt a little apart from my contemporaries, and always wanted to be recognized as a success by them, and indeed, over and above them, if I could manage it. So I slogged away at things I wasn't terribly good at, like playing cricket, to keep up with them, and to be accepted, and I studied comparatively thoroughly. I wasn't a great student or a great scholastic brain, but it seemed terribly important to me, I think for as long as I can remember, really.'

Sara Morrison, a Director of General Electric Company, saw aspects of her own later success as having roots in her early childhood. Although she was born into a socially privileged family, her childhood was recalled with mixed feelings. Like others in the group she suffered early parental loss and experienced an ambivalent relationship with her mother who after her father's death married again several times. When she was asked if she thought that her parents had greatly influenced her she answered, somewhat hesitantly: 'My father was killed when I was 10, during the war. And my mother? No. I did not want to be like her at all. At the time I did not think that she was a very happy person ... She married several times and had several step-daughters. Hence there was some degree of resentment on my part ... So as a child and young woman I viewed the world with a rather sceptical and slightly disenchanted glare ...

'I think it was this mixture of discontent, and not being very happy as a child, that stopped me in my later life from turning into someone who was at the vicarage arranging flowers or the President of the local Women's Institute: living worldlessly, waiting for her husband to come back from whatever, breeding dogs and bringing up the children. I can remember when I was 21, waking up one day, and saying "this may be me for the rest of my life. There has to be more to life than this!"'

She felt that her earlier painful experiences as a child had given her the strength and will to determine her own destiny and to launch out into an ambitious career in social work, politics and management. 'I could have continued leading a very selfish and self-indulgent life ... being asked to be President of everything, but not being allowed to run anything—the old sort of "squire-archy" existence! Instead, I was able to break out of the mould and prove that I could achieve something of my own. That gave me the greatest sense of achievement and satisfaction of my life!'

For others, a nomadic childhood meant that they lost the security of a permanent family life. They may have possessed the security of the family, but they also had the insecurity of constant mobility. In Sir Peter Parker's case the loss was more dramatic. One of his earliest childhood memories was of the family furniture, including his toys, being auctioned in a French street when his father was declared bankrupt. This was followed by a move to China, where he spent the remainder of his boyhood. Caught up in the Japanese-Chinese War in 1937, he lost not only his family belongings but also his two brothers, who were killed in the War. 'I was the youngest of three boys. My parents had settled in France after World War I, so I was born in France and spent my first seven years there. I suppose my first economic lesson was when my father, who was employed by a French company as an engineer, lost his work in the slump. So we had to sell up, and I remember the trick they have of selling all your furniture out on the street. That was an amazing thing—they auction it on the street, in front of the house. That was very interesting, my first "economic memory" really.

'Then we went to China—and father bravely went to China, no point in coming to Europe in the slump. He was English, a York-shireman, from Hull. When we got to China, to Shanghai, the Japanese-Chinese War was on, which was called "an incident" by the West, and we "came through" in China; my father did very well in China, he was a fine man. Of course China taught one a lot, because China was horrific. Millions in need, you know.' That this experience had made a vivid and lasting impression on the young child there was no doubt. He recalls vividly the sight of hordes of coolies, some no older than himself, unloading ships at the docks, many of them at the point of complete physical exhaustion and collapse. He remembers impossibly heavy loads being strapped to backs already red-raw with abrasions and open sores. 'We got about the country quite a bit, but father took a job on a ship for nine months and we lived very rough.

'But in '37, after six lovely years, we lost everything there. We were put on destroyers and rushed out as refugees to Hong Kong, because there was this so-called "incident" again—the Japanese-Chinese War.

'We lost everything in China, even the family photographs, which was serious because the War then broke out. Father had been abroad so long he could only go to Africa for a job, just before the War. He got a job there, then he couldn't call us out because the War started. Then both my brothers got killed in the War, and my mother was coping with me as a schoolboy, and then I got out of that and joined the Army. But we'd had a very good education. And so I came out of the War, very Left, and very anxious to steady up because I was furious with the smashing of the family and everything. I got engaged very young to a girl who married an American—great friends of ours still. I came out of the War and tried to get to Oxford just by buying a map at the station and walking round the colleges, knocking on doors. I got in before the end of the day; got three places. I had good fun, a marvellous time at Oxford. But all the time I was conscious that I had to try and understand why the world had been shaped that way.'

## REJECTION

Although the loss of a parent in childhood or in one's teens can have an adverse effect on the individual, and may shape the future, the experience of rejection by one's parents can be equally traumatic. John Harvey-Jones, Chairman of Imperial Chemical Industries, openly illustrates this. 'I was born in England, went out to India before I was one. Till the age of five I was brought up in a palace—my father was the Guardian of the Maharajah, an under-age one of about six years old.

'At the age of six I was brought home and put into an English prep school—boarding school—and that was it! My parents returned to India—I was just dumped! I'd not even seen traffic before, for instance. I'd never been in a large town. I remember when I was being taken to this prep school, being terrified as we travelled through London. When I arrived at the prep school, I'd absolutely no relevance at all to the sort of background that most of the other kids had—so I was miserable. I had a hell of a time. I wasn't a particularly robust child. I'm not doing a hearts and flowers thing, but I wasn't really happy until I joined the Navy.

'I was very fatherless. I was also to some extent without a

10

mother, because my mother again was out there most of the time. She was actually caught in the UK, she was meant to be returning to India in 1939, but the War came and caught her for the war years in England. But I was at sea from 1940, so again I saw very little of her. So I really had a very curious, almost orphan-like upbringing.

'I was an only child. I was a twin at one time, but my twin died very early—I grew up as an only child. And you know, there was just no ... I always wanted my father's approbation, which, incidentally, I never got. When I was decorated in the Navy, my father wasn't glowing ... I was decorated in a rather unusual way at a fairly young age, but I didn't get a bottle of champagne sent by my father, or an ecstatic telegram. Nothing! And I think that had some bearing on it.

'What I have felt is a continuing need to prove myself, and I developed that partly because of my experiences in my prep school, partly because of that feeling of being abandoned. Perhaps that's putting it a bit hot and strong, but I certainly felt "dumped"—I didn't feel I belonged to anybody.'

## FATHERS

In an earlier study in which a number of well-known actresses and women entertainers were interviewed about their success, it was found that their relationship with their fathers emerged as one of the most important factors in their drive to succeed. In strict Freudian terms, it is not surprising that the relationship between father and daughter is a fundamental building block to personality development and motivation for women. This influence may manifest itself in a number of ways: modelling a successful father; encouraging and promoting education for their daughters; where the father is absent through death or divorce, trying to meet imagined expectations; etc. It was surprising from our interviews to see the influence of the father, even among the men. We have already seen the importance of the father in the subsequent development of John Harvey-Jones. In that case the influence was of a negative sort, but still had a long-term significance and impact on the orientation and career of the chairman of one of the largest companies in Britain.

Sir Michael Edwardes, former Chairman of British Leyland and International Computers, and current Chairman of Chloride and Dunlop Holdings talking of his early home background and in particular the key influence of his father, told us: 'My parents didn't try to influence me. I could say I was sort of "turned loose" as it were, but could always get advice from either—my father was a fairly tough cookie—a typical sort of free enterprise chap.' In his autobiography he comments that he had 'had his own inevitable way of bringing up children. He saw life as an obstacle course and, as a part of their education, his children were required to practice on real, live obstacles'.

He recounts how at the age of 15 whilst on holiday at the family cabin disaster struck. Night fishing with a school friend some distance off shore, the outboard motor was lost overboard. After struggling back to the shore his father's reaction was entirely predictable to the young Michael Edwardes. The two boys were told that they would be left basic provisions and that they were staying at the cabin until they had recovered the lost motor. Eventually they found it after a full eight days of grappling and diving. (Michael Edwardes' first successful recovery!)

Michael Edwardes felt the lesson was clear and simple, 'You make your own mistakes and you correct them yourself. No-one looks after anyone from the cradle to the grave. If my father taught me anything it was that.' Finally he goes on to reflect on those early days: 'What was different about my early life? Perhaps that I wasn't spoon fed and that I was encouraged to get on with things.'

Lord Gormley, former President of the National Union of Mineworkers, was strongly influenced by his father, too. In defining his identity and role, he remarks: 'Two people were of great influence to me. My father was a great worker, he believed in working for his family. I was the middle of seven kids. He always provided for his family, but, like me, used to like a drink, like a bit of sport, he was a very good wrestler. He taught me (I don't know if I should use this term) how to be a MAN. I've a great regard for women—I think they go together. To be a man, you've got to

12

have a due regard for women, or females, or whatever you want to call them. The next one was my father-in-law. I had a wonderful father-in-law, and he was a great sportsman, a great companion. My mother, of course, naturally she was my biggest source of educated politics, because she was more of a politician than my dad. My dad was never involved in politics in the way that she was. She was the leader of the women's section. My wife's mother and my mother were founder members of the women's section, although I'd never met my wife properly until just a few months before we were married, but our families had been connected through our mothers. My dad was never a part of it—the politics. He was a Catholic, like myself, and mother was a bit of a devout Catholic, my father wasn't. He was very much like myself, and used to say, "Well, I go around doing the things which a good Christian should do. I see the best of everybody until I'm proved wrong. You don't need to go to church to prove that you're a good Christian," and I follow that belief as well.'

Lord Gormley's successor to the NUM Presidency was also strongly influenced by his father. Arthur Scargill was an only child, his father spending all his working life in the pits. From the early age of 12 he was taken by his father, an enthusiastic Communist, to local political meetings and rallies.

In an interview with *The Sunday Times* he stressed the influence his father had had upon his early development. 'He had more influence on me than anyone. Not directly—he never told me anything directly—but he read about eight books a week. The house was full of books: everything, the Bible, Shakespeare. My father still reads the dictionary every day! He says your life depends on your power to master words.'

The less direct but significant influence of the father can also be seen in the case of Clive Jenkins, General Secretary of the Association of Scientific, Technical and Managerial Staff: 'My father was a railway worker. He was a storekeeper and then a time-keeper on the Great Western railways. He got the job after being unemployed in the late 1920s–1930s in South Wales on that heavily industrialized south coast plain (Port Talbot), because my maternal grandfather was a railway foreman. He was an aristocrat, because he could hire and fire labour in those days and my memories of those days are of going to work with my father if he was on shift work, and handing out the brass tags to the engine drivers through the time-keeper's window and seeing very strong black tea brewed on top of the stove. I can still remember the smell of the grease and the very special waste materials they used to use for polishing down the engines, because the engines were all polished then, particularly their brass.'

Some fathers strongly encouraged their subsequently notable sons and daughters to achieve success in education as a means to ultimate success. Jeremy Isaacs reflected: 'I had two brothers, and we were encouraged to get the best out of our education, and out of our lives. We were given the sense that it was possible for us to do so, I don't think it is so possible for many of today's young people to do this. To both please their parents and to challenge them by greater achievements in education than particularly my father had had to find for himself. So that nothing made himself happier than our success.'

Elizabeth MacDonald, Marketing Director of Knight, Frank and Rutley, was particularly encouraged by her father. While she was growing up her father was working seven days a week and her mother, while providing a background of love and security, was very occupied in bringing up her four children. So she was encouraged towards self-sufficiency and independence. 'I would say that in terms of assets in the way in which I was brought up, I had a most unusual father. He was an incredibly independent person, most unconventional and wouldn't be considered a success in terms of making lots of money because he was a bricklayer for his whole life. But his approach would be very much that one should question everything and never accept what other people had told you or what was written down, but to do your own homework and assess it for yourself. It just rings in my ears, throughout my upbringing, "Look into it yourself, find out, and you decide." I wasn't ever told how to go about things, but encouraged to make a list of the pros and cons and make my own decision, from the beginning, about anything. My father was most reluctant to give people advice—he'd rather they should choose. I think it is a help if you have had that sort of background.'

It was surprising that one or two of the group tended to model their fathers' entrepreneurial and executive skills. This could be seen in the account by Prue Leith, Managing Director of Prudence Leith Enterprises and Board Director of British Rail, of her relationship with her parents, which was reflected in her own business success. 'I was born in South Africa, into a typical middle class white South African family, very privileged. My father was a director of a subsidiary of ICI, and he was a businessman, and a very good one, and my mother was an actress, a top actress (she was South Africa's great actress and producer of the time). So I grew up with her being very famous and my father being very successful.

'I had a fantastically happy childhood, I adored them both, my father more than my mother, I suppose, because I suppose there's a natural affinity between fathers and daughters, but I suppose I also saw less of him and more of my mother.

'I never remember my parents quarrelling, they must have quarrelled, but they did it behind closed doors if they did, and I never remember anybody raising a voice. In a way we were governed by disapproval, which I can remember getting very resentful about at one point. It was awful not to be the apple of my father's eye, and when we were behaving badly, it made him unhappy that we were badly behaved and so he would be a bit sour, and withdraw his affection in a way, and really if we were governed at all, it was by disapproval.'

Jonathan Miller, the TV and Theatrical Director and Producer, was also greatly influenced by his parents, particularly his father. His mother was a writer, and his father, a highly successful psychiatrist, one of the pioneers of child guidance (and founder of the *Journal of Child Psychiatry*). His father, who was a particularly strong influence on Jonathan Miller's subsequent drive and success, was also very interested in philosophy, sculpture and painting. So with all this, and his mother's literary background, Miller reflects: 'My background was rather academic and heavy. A professional, academic, a rather achievement-orientated world. My father was scholarly, multilingual and multidisciplinary. That was the sort of network into which I was born and I was pulled very quickly into different ways. A sort of context grid of interests.'

As we will see in a later chapter, Jonathan Miller subsequently attempted to emulate his father's success in medicine by becoming a doctor and continues to be keenly concerned with medical science and research.

Mary Quant, of Mary Quant Group, was similarly encouraged by both her parents: 'I think that my parents were ambitious for their children and found it important. They made it clear that one had to earn one's living, so do it in something you enjoy doing— the best thing in life is to actually get paid for something you enjoy doing.'

**MOTHERS**

Although many of our 'change makers' mentioned their mothers less frequently than their fathers in the context of their drive to succeed, we noticed that in several cases mothers played a subtle and indirect role in influencing their career aspirations. Although Prue Leith became an entrepreneur, as her father had been, she secretly admired her mother's success as an actress. At one point she followed in her mother's footsteps by attending drama school, but ultimately entered the world of business like her father. Her ambivalence towards the 'female role' in society is nicely summed up: 'I used to complain that my mother didn't make cakes for the school fête, and never turned up to watch me being Ratty and Moley in "Toad of Toad Hall", because she was always working. And I'm very proud of the fact that she was famous, and my big day came when she came to talk at the school about the theatre, and then I felt 20 feet off the ground, because I had such a famous mother. But there were times when I thought she was absolutely no good at all. She was too glamorous and too good looking, and her clothes were too young, and I wanted her to be fat and make cakes and stand behind the stall on fête day, and stuff like that.'

Although Sir Michael Edwardes focused mainly upon the role his father played in his early development, his mother Audrey was also a strong, if less direct influence. Like many white South African women with time on their hands, she was much involved with committees and 'good causes'. Edwardes' younger sister, Gill, a director of a leading advertising agency in Johannesburg, said in a *Sunday Times* interview that Mrs Edwardes was an incisive,

witty woman who 'absolutely sublimated her brain in bridge ...
she was also an appalling snob. We were brought up to believe
we were God's gift to the world. We were both highly motivated,
"achievers".'

Raised by his mother and grandmother in a tight matriarchal
environment, Richard Ingrams acknowledged that both women
had played a major role in his early development. He was very
close to his mother and as the youngest son he enjoyed a special
relationship with her. He felt she was particularly influential in
encouraging a belief in the Church, a belief which is still active
today. 'My mother was influential in two key ways. The first a
religious one, she was a staunch Roman Catholic. She was also a
very keen musician. Her two interests really were religion and
music.'

Interest in literature and in writing was encouraged by his
grandmother, who came from a literary family, and had been a
close friend of G.K. Chesterton. Ingrams remembers the house
being full of his books and as a young child he became engrossed
in his work.

Parental influences are not always positive. Lord Longford,
former Leader of the House of Lords and Director of Sidgwick
& Jackson, tells how his father left for the front during the First
World War when he was nine, and never returned. He was killed
in action and Lord Longford was then brought up by his mother.
'The truth is that my mother was not very cordial towards me.
My elder brother she adored and always did so. I think I would
have to say that I could never satisfy my mother. So if I suffer
from any kind of neurosis, it is largely because I was unable to
live up to her expectations ... Someone might explain my character in this way.'

On the other hand, Jeremy Isaacs' positive attitude towards his
mother can be seen in the following comment. 'My father kept a
small jeweller's shop and my mother was a doctor, in the south
side of Glasgow. I have a huge regard for her. I think that it was
not easy to be a doctor in the days she was. She couldn't drive a
car for years, but even when she did, when she got to the house
that she had to make the call in she would have to walk up four
or five flights of stairs in the tenements of the south side.'

## SIGNIFICANT OTHERS

Parents were not the only influence on the individuals in our group. Some of these prominent people were influenced by well-known figures of their time. Clive Jenkins, for example, illustrates this: 'I had joined the Labour Party when I was 14 under the influence of all sorts of artistic and cultural activities which went on during the War. A school teacher again helped to set up something called "The Forum" where you had debates. They were very popular—people didn't have much else to do in between all the war work—and they'd occasionally take a large chapel and invite a guest speaker down. That's when I met Julian Huxley, for example. So there was I at 15 actually having tea with Julian Huxley—just due to the activities of this little intellectual group which used to try to collect signatures, for example, in one case to get a civil list pension for a poet, and I think only in South Wales would you get small boys like me going from door to door saying "Now, will you sign this petition for a civil list pension for this poet!" I met Joad, who came down, Desmond Bernard, who came down, so this excited all sorts of things. The local Co-op Insurance manager gave me two books, I remember, an introduction to Marx and Machiavelli. Never looked back!'

As we discussed earlier, Arthur Scargill continues to be influenced by the memory of his mother. Len Murray, who also lost his mother when he was relatively young, seemed to transfer his maternal relationship to his auntie—whom he regards as having had a significant influence in terms of education: 'I had a hard fight to survive in school, and I'll say this for my auntie, that she was absolutely intent on me getting an education. If she hadn't been there I'd have left school. The idea was I'd stay on my uncle's farm and so on and work there. She was very influential in developing my education.'

Murray was also influenced by his local doctor, who opened his library to him and encouraged him to read the great writers of the time. In addition, he was encouraged by his English master at school, who had the capacity to bring subjects to life for the young Murray, particularly about far-away places.

## EDUCATION

It also became clear that education, in one form or another, was crucial to most of those we interviewed. Many of them spent an inordinate amount of time talking about their early education and the influence this had on their attitudes and subsequent success. As you will recall, for example, Jeremy Isaacs talked about the influence of being evacuated to Kirkcudbrightshire in south-west Scotland, and the fact that being Jewish in rural Scotland meant that he felt he had to try that bit harder to impress his contemporaries. He worked hard at sport and academic life, even though he felt he was not 'a great student or scholastic brain'. But this drive to prove himself in the eyes of his contemporaries seemed less easily achieved during further education: 'I went to various grand Glasgow schools, Glasgow High School and Glasgow Academy, and I found that although in some ways I wanted an ethos I needed to argue with the ethos of the schools—particularly of the Academy, which was a very toffee-nosed public school—anyone in charge of Glasgow went—and I was on the left of that. Nevertheless, I did use the school to the greatest benefit I could derive from it. Getting to the top of the school in various ways, in the Cadet Corps, in the cricket team, as a prefect, and then I won a scholarship to the University of Oxford. It was in a discipline which actually, I knew I wasn't very good at, and I didn't particularly enjoy. The reason I was doing it was that it was the likeliest one to get me assisted entry to Oxford! That was Classics. And so I read Greek, catching up with other people who'd been studying before I got round to it, and Latin, and I enjoyed English and History and French more than either Latin or Greek, but it was on a Latin Classics scholarship that I got to Merton College, Oxford. I was going to do my National Service before university, but was told by the College that my Classics was a bit shaky, and that I ought to come up straight away. So I filled in another two terms at school and then went up to Oxford. Still trying to achieve, and knowing (I think) that I was not going to achieve it in a discipline in which I was not expert. I realized as soon as I got there that while I had perhaps been the brightest boy in Glasgow Academy's very small Sixth Form, in terms of Latin and Greek,

I was one of hundreds studying the subject at Oxford. I was against the brightest of Eton, Winchester, St Paul's and everywhere else. So I started other things that I enjoyed and was interested in. I joined the Labour Club, played football (wasn't very good at that, but still, I insisted on doing it!). I rather tried to do too much at Oxford, but I enormously enjoyed it and got a very great deal out of it.'

Prue Leith, on the other hand, tried a number of different educational routes before settling on cookery almost by chance. Unlike Jeremy Isaacs, she was not under any peer or parental pressure, and was able to experiment with different potential career choices, first drama, then art, and then languages. 'I spent all my childhood in South Africa, I was at school in Johannesburg, and university at Cape Town. I flunked out of university. I thought I wanted to be an actress, because my mother was, I suppose, and because I'm something of an egotist. But then when I got to drama school I found that I didn't really like it—I liked the play-reading and I liked the research and I liked the rehearsals. I didn't like the actual performance, I was absolutely terrified. So then I swopped to art school, because I thought I'd do stage design because I still wanted to be around the stage, and I didn't last very long in art school because they said, quite correctly, that I couldn't draw! So then, I thought, well perhaps I would get academic, so I started doing a BA.

'The funny thing about Cape Town was I was always still at the university. I always was doing an art course at university, but I kept changing what I was doing, from drama to design to ... And then I thought seriously I'd get a BA, and my father was absolutely thrilled. And then I flunked French. What had happened was that in my second year I was so convinced that I hadn't done any work I did the first three exams and I thought "well, I've failed them so there's no point in turning up for the next three". And of course, I had passed the first three ... I did the classic thing of flunking out for no good reason. So then I said to my poor parents, who were sick to death of the whole story by now, that I wanted to go to France, because I was very interested in French, and I'd only learn to speak French if I went abroad and overseas etc. I think all South Africans long to come to Europe because they feel so away from it all. So I went to the Sorbonne to do their Civilization Course (so called), and it was when I was in Paris that I got hooked on food. I mean, I was an au pair student, working for a family, and I got very keen on food.'

For Len Murray, his education was strongly influenced by the encouragement and support of his ex-headmaster. 'My headmaster said "What do you want to do?" I didn't have much sympathy with him. He said "You need to get yourself trained properly." "Yes, I suppose I do. Where do I go?" "Go to Oxford." You know, me in the middle of Wellington High Street on a Saturday morning being told to go to Oxford. So he sends me some papers about it, entrance examinations, etc. I swotted, worked nights and Saturday mornings and so on, and the college accepted me. So, if I hadn't walked down that particular street, on that particular morning, would I be sitting here—probably the answer is no! Somebody else would be sitting here. So all my experiences and wishes and ambitions congeal together in one moment. Oh, Oxford to me was a polytechnic. There were certain subjects to study and certain skills to acquire and I treated it as a training institution. Not like all the other fellows—real inspired and all the rest of it, but I knew what I wanted.'

Clive Jenkins was similarly encouraged by his school teachers to go further: 'In South Wales when you were adopted by a school teacher you realized they were rather special people. Some of them would present their own prizes, they'd buy books. I remember winning a prize when I was in the fourth form of the junior school. I was looked after then. I can identify at least four teachers who took special care and sent you postcards about details of archaeological sites when they went abroad. I'd never been abroad so it was all very exciting. They were very kind. The tragedy with one, I remember, he went off to the War, and became a pilot and was shot down and killed. I missed him for quite a while.'

As far as the female 'change makers' are concerned, the attitudes towards women pursuing further education and careers had a major impact. Elizabeth MacDonald recalls: 'My three brothers had very long educations but it was felt that someone needed to help the family finances and I was judged to be the one who least needed a long education for two reasons—girls from working class backgrounds usually tend to marry fairly young, so it was thought that I would get married, and alternatively, even if I didn't marry, I could probably cope better without a long formal education than some other people, but I wouldn't have chosen to stop my formal education at sixteen.'

During the time that most of these women were pursuing their secondary and university education, the norms were single-sex schools and few women in higher education. Clare Mulholland, Deputy Director of Television Independent Broadcasting Authority, not only had to overcome the obstacles of wanting to pursue a male career path in terms of education, but also had to overcome the barriers faced by girls from the working class. 'I went to Notre Dame High School, which was the best of the Catholic girls' day schools. My parents were obviously interested in education. Neither of them had been able to stay on at school. With hindsight I can see that was a very strong influence on us, that they encouraged us, because they wanted us to have the opportunities they had not had. But it was never in a strict way. It was simply there as an encouragement. But it did mean there was no attempt on my parents' part to influence us as to what we did—whether we stayed on for higher education or not. Simply because they didn't know enough about it. So there was encouragement to stay on, and I suppose to do well, but there was no possibility of discussing with them when it came to thinking about university, because they didn't know.'

She told us that she did not use her time at university to pursue the conventional programme of academic study. Rather, like Prue Leith, she explored newly found interests, often outside the university setting. It was for her a time of reflection, of a developing political awareness and of a growing and lasting realization of the role of women within society.

'So at university I was interested in doing other things, I was interested in debating, I suppose always having been a bit argumentative, but again no strong political interest. I started off by joining the Scottish National Party, because my approach was very emotional; I think I thought that Scotland got a bad deal. After a year I changed and joined the Liberal Party, who were then undergoing a revival, and I stayed with the Liberals when I was a student and did debates (they have parliamentary debates in Glasgow). I debated in both the Women's Union and the Men's Union. They have separate unions—women are graciously permitted to enter the debates (and for dances!). So I did a lot of things outside—mainly to do with debates. To me the experience of university was the stimulus of that, and the privilege of having time to spend doing just that. By the end of the time I knew that I didn't want to stay in Glasgow (I found it too restrictive as a society then). Partly I thought that women were regarded as second class citizens, not as students, but it seemed to me in the work place they tended to be. And secondly, it was too narrow, and I didn't like the sectarian religious background at all. I found it simply absurd, and didn't really want to be part of that—I just wanted to move. But I think the only career ambition I had was a negative one—I did not want to be a teacher!'

Despite the variations in both experience of, and attitudes toward, the formal educational system, almost all of our 'change makers' saw their years of full time education as providing an opportunity to experiment with their own ideas and interests rather than as following a conventional educational career. Even at this stage they were stamping their individuality upon the established social institution.


## CONCLUSION

Much of the material in this chapter illustrates the influence of formative early experiences on the personality development of our successful 'change makers'. While recognizing the inherent dangers of *post-hoc* conclusions, we feel it was significant that many of those we interviewed emphasized the importance of childhood experiences. Memories of loss, whether of person or place, and feelings of insecurity, were recalled vividly, and often with emotion, by many of the group and were often held to be a significant factor in their later development. Psychologists might see these early adverse experiences as likely to be traumatic, literally 'wounding' to the developing personality. Yet, as the physical wound produces a healthy scar tissue often stronger than normal to protect the damaged area, so the personality may protect itself by defending vulnerable aspects of the psyche in similar ways, by compensating through a number of defence mechanisms. Certainly, a number of those we interviewed reported feelings of *strength through adversity*. This was often guided and directed by some 'significant other person' to the achievement of some positive goals. Early traumas seemed to have resulted in a successful testing out of their 'survival skills', a 'psychic tempering', leading to a basic feeling of strength, self-sufficiency and independence, which would serve them well in their later careers.

As might be expected, parental influences in particular were crucial during those formative years. The influence of the father was particularly highlighted. The father, although often identified as a somewhat remote and distant figure, seems particularly important in providing a role model, which consciously or unconsciously many of the members of our group tried to emulate. Indeed, he was a key factor in their drive to succeed. The mother was a more subtle influence, remembered in terms of providing the elements of security and encouragement, that is, *enabling* their children to succeed. As individuals they also showed an inherent curiosity about the world at large, with voracious appetites for reading and knowledge generally.

It is also interesting to note the marginal nature of many of our 'change makers', in terms of mainstream British society. It can be seen that many of them came from minority religious groups, or from abroad or were raised abroad. They were on the fringes of various majority groups, in what psychologists colloquially refer to as 'boundary roles'. Could it be that adverse life experiences, together with their marginal role in society were motivating forces to achieve establishment positions? Or is it an attempt to impose order on what appears to be an 'unjust world', that is, to regain control over their own destiny?

# CHAPTER TWO

# SYSTEMS
# OF BELIEF

*'A man like me cannot live without a hobby-horse, a consuming passion—
in Schiller's words a* tyrant. *I have my tyrant, and in his service I know no
limits. My tyrant is psychology.'*

Sigmund Freud

## I BELIEVE

Though most of our 'change makers' considered themselves essentially as individualistic operators, they also saw their actions as
part of a much wider philosophical perspective. Without exception, they have well-developed and clearly articulated value and
belief systems in which their own actions are precisely located.
These beliefs not only provide direction and purpose, but also
justification and support when they come under pressure.

Running through almost all of the interviews was a strong sense
of spirituality, a belief in something, whether an organized religion, or a consciousness of something more important or meaningful outside oneself. Christianity in its broadest sense obviously
had meaning for Len Murray, Lord Gormley, Clive Jenkins,
Richard Ingrams and Lord Longford.

Lord Gormley, for example, highlights the influence of Catholicism: 'I'm a Catholic, but you don't have to go to church. I'm not saying it in a derogatory way, but I think I do act as a Christian, and I would still only act in that way if I went to church. I might think if I went to church that it solves all accounts, but it doesn't, you see, so I tend to act as a Christian and I wouldn't do a bad thing to anybody. Plus, as you go along in life, and see what's happening—the problems that have been caused in the world in the name of religions, make me acutely angry!'

Len Murray reflects on his Methodist background: 'Remember when you consider my actions I am a Christian. Remember I look beyond this—I certainly don't look for "Heaven on Earth", but as much of an approximation as you can get—that's a bit Buddhist really. So that it is a very powerful influence on my behaviour.

'I wasn't of the faith at all. I came into the Methodist Church, where I am now, through the East End, when I was living in London. And seeing the Church, that Church, in action; dealing with the casualties that the welfare state missed out completely, the people were so filthy, they couldn't even go to a doctor's surgery because they were kept out—people wouldn't have them sitting by them, etc.'

Lord Longford saw himself as 'a practising Christian'. 'Everything I do would be related to that fact. It makes it easy. It's like the Marxist [who] would be relating it all to what Karl Marx said. I relate everything to what Christ said. It puts *everything* into a perspective for me.'

And Clive Jenkins on his Welsh Calvinist Methodism: 'It's a sort of Methodist teaching/preaching compulsion. I was also a lay preacher on Sundays ... there was a temperance group for young people and we used to supply preachers if one of the local ones, or one of the ones on the circuit couldn't turn up. So I used to go up the mountains and speak in the tin-roofed bethanies. That was interesting, because you had a chance to address yourself in sentences to audiences as preaching Christian Socialism, but that had an effect on me. I didn't drink until I was 25—probably drink too much now! It's a reliever of stress—a bit of a reflex I suppose, but I didn't drink until I was 25, but then I think this was the Welsh Calvinistic drive, and others have it, you can recognize it in other people—they're the ones that never really relax. They've always got a goblin on their shoulder saying "Why aren't you working and preferably perspiring?".'

For some it is an awareness of their own integrity and the need to safeguard their self-respect that is all important in their career. John Harvey-Jones is ambivalent about the outcomes of success. 'I don't know anybody who has really been improved by success.' Pressed on his own internal standards, he told us that 'One of the personal things that I have set myself is to realize that I will have to live with myself when I leave this job. And I am desperately intent to preserve my integrity as a person. I don't mean that in any sort of holy sense. Quite simply I want to preserve my "fullness" as a person so that I leave this job, hopefully, the same sort of person that started it, and ideally a little bit better. That is very important to me.'

Lord Weinstock and Elizabeth MacDonald, on the other hand, have described their belief systems in more generic terms. Lord Weinstock emphasizes the spirituality 'within': 'I don't subscribe to a formal religion ... I don't think that religion as enshrined in the procedures of the different churches is a thing to believe in. No human being can say "I know there is no force outside the observable human universe" as a statement of objective fact, you cannot know what is not known—it is not possible. I think also on balance there is certainly some force or something, not something, but there are force or forces which are a great deal more potent than I am. If you think of the lack of potency in any human being, I don't care who, in the face of real power in the world, even the power of a storm, or the sea getting rough, or something like that, the natural forces in the universe ... stand on top of a power station if you really want to feel trivial. There it is producing 500 megawatts under you, it gives one a feeling of having no consequence whatsoever. I think that the words religion and belief are the problem. I am conscious of something, which would not be called formal religion, but I perhaps have the same idea of religion as Abraham had seeing God in the burning bush. There is no church between the two and in so far as I feel that there is a moral responsibility to something maybe inside me as well as outside me, I have a religious belief.'

Elizabeth MacDonald raises the issue of the purpose of life

generally: 'One has to go back to what one perceives as the purpose in life and I think that life is primarily about spiritual development, I think that is what we are striving towards. So that would be a big influence on my life, so I would always be striving to develop in some way that I could. One doesn't always need pleasant experiences to develop, so I don't expect to have a marvellous time, but I hope to have an interesting time and the fact that I like working so much is perhaps a reflection that I find it an easy field in which to develop further.'

There are others for whom the politics of life are their central core. For Arthur Scargill, Socialism and the underlying beliefs of Christianity are inextricably linked.

'Someone I regard as a very great leader is Fidel Castro, and I think Castro has all the qualities one could wish to see in an individual leader, with his roots firmly based in the working class movement of Cuba, and Fidel has always said that wherever there is a problem, and Cuba's assistance is required—then it is not a question of whether or not we help; but a question of Cuba having an obligation to help another socialist who is in trouble. And equally I see in our movement in Britain that we have an obligation to help others who are in difficulties. If the nurses are struggling they are least able to help themselves and we have an obligation to come to their assistance. So there are, if you like, comparisons that can be made on the national and international scale in politics with the things that you find in the trade union movement.'

Addressing the Cambridge University Union in 1975, Arthur Scargill told them that his ultimate task was to change society and that, he added, 'is why we create conflict'.

'If I wasn't optimistic about the future of man I wouldn't be a socialist. If I wasn't optimistic about the future of Socialism and mankind I don't think I'd want this job either. I've absolute faith in mankind. Even if they throw me out of this job tomorrow, it doesn't mean the people are wrong. If I lose the national presidency, it doesn't mean the people are wrong, it doesn't mean the miners are wrong. What it does mean is they can be influenced by all the features I've talked about previously, and they can be influenced to such an extent they make the wrong decisions, as indeed the people in Germany did before the Second World War. But it doesn't make people wrong, it makes individuals practise wrong things at certain times; it makes wrong decisions possible, but I believe that man inherently is good. I think there is nothing to prevent people building a better world in which to live, and I think that as I read so many years ago, that we should see a world without war, we shall see a world without want, and I have no doubt in my mind that this can become a reality, sooner rather than later.'

## WHAT FUNCTION DOES IT SERVE?

*'It is important for everyone to believe, whether they succeed or not, that success is linked with some kind of logic and beholden to some notion of legitimacy ... To put it another way, it is psychologically intolerable, having risen to the heights, to be badgered by doubt that you do not really deserve it.'*

Alistair Mant

For many of the group their belief system provided both a sense of purpose and justification. Several talked of a powerful sense of 'fate'. For Lord Gormley 'there were just so many coincidences'. He felt that they were almost part of a grander order or design: 'To get to be President [of the NUM] there has been a lot of coincidences. I've been aware of these throughout my life. If I had not lost the election for General Secretary, I couldn't have been elected President two years later, and the presidency is a much more powerful position. It makes you feel that fate somehow has destined you to have this position of authority. It seemed ordained that all this would happen. So, whatever the problems I have to face, I'm fatalistic in my belief that it will turn out for the best.'

Len Murray had the same feeling about coincidences. As he recalled earlier, a chance meeting with his ex-headmaster in the main street of his home town led to a successful scholarship application to Oxford. 'The question is, if I hadn't been walking down that particular street in a Shropshire market town on that particular Saturday morning, would I be here now? And the

29

probable answer is *no*! Really, it could be any other person sat behind that desk. That is a great consolation as it induces a certain modesty and humility. Why have you come to see me? Not because of me, but because I'm part of something bigger. Because I'm the General Secretary. Because I represent the TUC.'

Sir Peter Parker made a point of stressing the importance of a well-worked-out system of values as a guide to effective decision making. Quoting Johnson's comment that 'nothing so much needs a philosophy than business,' he stressed that managerial action must be grounded in a well-developed philosophy of action, of cause and effect. In his view a clearly thought out idea of purpose and values together with professional skills and abilities were the hallmarks of the successful manager.

His own 'belief system', which, he told us, has guided both his past and present career, revolves around one of his most strongly held views—the social responsibility of commerce and industry. Forcefully reiterating principles that guided the Quaker 'captains of industry' a century ago, Sir Peter Parker believes that business organizations must become more aware of their impact upon their locality and upon society in general.

He expounded in some detail those influences which had helped him form his own philosophy of life and the place of business in society. 'I believe strongly in the social function of business ... It is industry which creates our social patterns, it determines the whole form of our society, whether it is education or the design of cities. And I am concerned with the splits that I see in industry as they run right out into the fabric of our society.'

Ideologically, he is a champion of the 'mixed economy'—where State interests and private enterprise exist in a mutually beneficial 'symbiotic' relationship. 'I am myself the mixed economy man par excellence,' he told *Spectator* readers in 1980. 'I have always recognized how imperative it is to reconcile business efficiency with pluralistic democratic pressures.' This belief has guided both his actions and his thinking and has led to a totally pragmatic approach. 'From the left I borrow the ideals of participation and social awareness, and from the right the key concepts of profitability and marketing!'

When he advocates the 'social objectives' of management he is not only concerned with achieving a delicate balance between what at first sight appears to be irreconcilable forces, of public and private enterprise, of union and management interests, of capitalism and social equality, but rather with the introduction of a new professionalism in management. A 'new look' management which has an accepted social dimension and a duty to look beyond the narrow confines of the balance sheet and the shareholders' report.

That he has been able to put these principles into operation successfully is evidenced by Barbara Castle's comments upon his style of leadership. 'His is a magical mixture: a tough management mind coupled with a sensitivity towards individuals, an optimistically determined man.'

Sir Peter Parker went on to comment, in somewhat mystical terms, that his philosophy not only guided but also provided the confidence and ultimate justification for his actions. 'After a while you begin to trust your energy and belief, and you find yourself becoming more and more confident about it. I feel in a sense—it's very complicated that business when one tries to explain oneself, one usually always talks about not the real drives, which are unspeakable, but one comes out with some fancy talk. But really, if you have a view about life, or about death, which is probably equally as important, you do sense that there is something which you won't be able to explain at any point. But you are conscious whatever talents you have, that when you are at your best, there is something bigger than that working, and you begin to trust, some spiritual energy is with you. You find yourself confident about it and you find, in fact, sometimes if you're doing something really very good, you suddenly realize, "Well, it isn't me doing it". You feel, "My God, just do it", and you do it. Then somebody says, "Why did you do that?", and you think "Christ, why did I do it?" But you know that you're doing the right thing and you just have done it.'

For Lord Weinstock, this philosophy was rooted in the Protestant ethic and the use of logic: 'It is a struggle. Not a shooting match, but a battle with others; others who you do not hate, but who are struggling for the same thing. In order to get what we want we have to deny it to someone else. In the role of Chairman I have a very specific job to do. Because I work in a free enterprise system, choices are limited, but the use of logic will lead me to the best choice.'

Arthur Scargill was equally firm about his position within his particular organization, which he preferred to think of as 'the cause'. Identification with a cause or belief provides a vehicle through which the individual can achieve both self-expression and personal identity. Its loss can have disastrous consequences. 'If I commit myself to anything, it is a hundred per cent, there can be no half measures. If it is to an organization, to an ideal, to a political philosophy, or to people, it is one hundred per cent. The subsequent loss, or the effects of the loss, of severing that connection can be quite dramatic. I remember when I was kicked out of the Young Communist League and the devastating effect it had on me.

'I found that, for the first time since the age of 14, I was no longer able to have the central organization to communicate with. I could not pose questions which would get some kind of collective reflection. I felt very isolated and (in spite of being a loner), it took a very long time to adjust to that isolation. What would happen if I lost my job? I don't know. It is so much a part of me that it would be a very traumatic experience indeed.'

Richard Ingrams illustrated the support and strength he found in his religious convictions when he experienced a traumatic experience of loss. 'I was very influenced ten years ago when we had a handicapped child, who is now dead. That influenced my life in a very powerful way, some good ways, some bad. Up to the time that happened my life had been fairly easy-going. Everything suddenly changed. Ordinary people do not realize what a terrific burden it is.'

He was able to talk about the effects on both his family and himself and how it strengthened his religious convictions. 'Obviously it does put a great strain on the whole family. In a way it is disruptive but, as Malcolm Muggeridge would say, a sense of suffering of any form can ultimately be a beneficial thing. It is painful but I believe it is true. Through it I came to a much deeper appreciation of life and what it is all about.

'It also has had an effect on my religious beliefs. It forces you to think about life. I find myself taking a much more positive attitude towards Christianity.

'I did not turn to religion, as I have always had this belief. I was brought up in a very strongly religious setting. My mother is a Roman Catholic. There has always been a powerful influence on me in an indirect way. So in a sense I had that already.

'It is more the effect of having normal children growing up that makes you think about religion because you have to really think about what you believe in and not what you want your children to believe in. An incident like this forces you to relive your life again, to go back and ask "What do I believe in?", and that is a very healthy process.'

Overall it is apparent that each member of our group has a very well defined belief system which orders their reality. The pay-off is considerable. One must look with some admiration at the clarity of action and purpose which such a sense of mission imparts. No doubt, in the terms of the eminent American psychologist George Kelly, a set of clear 'core-constructs' gives this clarity. Certainly a basic belief in the rightness of one's actions alleviates problems of what psychologists term 'cognitive dissonance', i.e. the need to feel psychologically at ease with one's decisions.

However, the potentiality for action thus engendered can obviously be used for a variety of ends, and it is a moot point as to where exactly the dividing line lies between clarity of purpose and narrowness of purpose, between enthusiasm and fanaticism, between open and closed minds. Single-mindedness in the pursuit of a central cause may mark the successful 'change maker', but narrowness of vision is what bigotry is made of.


**CONCLUSION**

It can be seen that many of the members of our group had a strong sense of mission, a deep-seated belief system or as Sir Francis Drake reflected on his own personality, 'a sword in one hand, a Bible in the other and a good eye to the main chance'. In addition, each individual had an idiosyncratic structure of beliefs: some were religious, others were politically inspired, others motivated for the 'greater good' and still others by a strong belief in their own ability (or as Petula Clark reflected in *Public Faces*,

*Private Lives*, 'I feel that one has got to be strong in one's self; it's got to be like a steel cord going all the way through, and it's just got to be there. You've got to have that invisible courage running through you like steel.').

This system of belief seems to serve a number of different purposes. It could provide them with control or direction or security or a *raison d'être* for their activities. It seems that the loss, separation, rejection or adverse life experience may encourage them to seek some secure foundation in a belief system. What they have lost in childhood, they gain in their allegiance to a substantive structure of beliefs, be it Christianity or Socialism or concern for the homeless. It is interesting that few if any of the individuals interviewed held extreme or radical views (i.e. were anarchists or Moonies). In the main, they held *established* systems of belief, which leads us to feel that they may be in need of an established identity, that is, permanent roots. This may provide them with an integrity of the personality (i.e. of the self) absent because of loss, or negative experiences in the formative years. Indeed, the supra-ordinate belief system may serve a crucial dual function. On the one hand, it compensates for the deprivations in early years, whilst providing them with a stable foundation for their future activities, in what is likely to be an insecure and risky work environment.

# CHAPTER THREE

# LONERS

*'The whole theory of the universe is directed unerringly to one single individual—namely to you.'*

Walt Whitman

While we had expected to find 'change makers' rather solitary individuals, isolated from lesser mortals by their position and role, we had not expected to find that this isolation was an essential factor which could be traced like an unbroken thread running through childhood and adolescence.

Indeed, perhaps the strongest attribute to emerge from the whole group is that of being 'a loner'. It is a keystone of their personality, often clearly identifiable in childhood and later life, exhibited as a strong sense of independence and self-reliance. 'Change makers', it seems, march to the 'beating of a private and inner drum'. As individuals they seem to be, at the one time, part of and yet separate from, mainstream society. They seem to maintain a delicate balance between a public and a private existence, between involvement in social concern on the one hand, and relaxing into their own self-sufficiency on the other; the ultimate paradox of the individual operating in a social setting.

This self-containment seems well recognized and accepted by them. Often, as might be expected from the evidence presented in Chapter 1, its origins go back to early childhood. Usually it is maintained through adolescence. An adolescence marked by few friends and rather solitary pursuits. So it remains into adulthood where it is regarded as a major personality trait, and a desirable one at that. To overstate the case, it seems that whilst society might have need of them, they do not feel they need society to the same degree.

Prue Leith, talking about her early catering venture, said she led a somewhat solitary existence. She had no relatives in this country and lived alone in London. 'I am the sort of person who just loves being alone. I remember the pleasure of my first bedsitter in Earl's Court. It was up two or three flights of incredibly stinking stairs ... the whole place was disgusting. But it was mine and I could find the space and solitude I've always needed.'

Lord Longford puts it like this: 'Yes, I am very much a loner in this sphere [initiating change]. I have a wide circle of social acquaintances, but these are not close friends. I only have a few really close friends.

'I am not a loner in my private life. I am happily married with lots of children and grandchildren, but I am a loner in trying to bring about change. In change, yes, you must be a loner.

'I do initiate change. I start up an inquiry into something entirely off my own bat. At first I got no support from anywhere. My wife may say, "Yes, it sounds like a jolly good idea," but the idea is mine and I am totally responsible for it.

'So I think on the whole anyone who is an individual agent of change and who is involved in this sort of [social] change must be, by definition, a loner. I certainly am.'

Questioned further on how this particular style developed, Lord Longford linked it directly with early expressions of rejection and disappointment that he experienced in earlier life. Even within his own aristocratic milieu he had felt deprived and excluded. As a young child he was rejected by his mother, and, as a second eldest son, saw his father's title, estates and considerable fortune passed to his elder brother. He found himself disadvantaged in a privileged world. Even in his family home in Ireland he had 'always seemed a bit of an outsider' and felt unable to support the Irish cause in the vocal way that guaranteed his brother's local popularity.

As an individual he seems to locate himself on the edge of society, and readily admits to a feeling of 'being an outcast'. Although he takes some pride in his label of 'the outcasts' outcast' ('I hope that could be put on my tombstone!'), he sees himself rather as 'the champion of neglected causes'. Causes in which individuals are often 'the powerless victims of society', and which he as an individual, and as a loner, can effect some degree of alleviation and change.

Uncharacteristically of their occupation, perhaps, three of the trade union representatives expressed some pride in their feelings of solitariness. Arthur Scargill said: 'I must say this, I've always been a bit of a loner. A loner both inside and outside of the working group. I do see myself as a loner, though I think that there is a distinct difference between being a loner and loneliness. I am not lonely, I could have thousands of friends. But I do prefer solitude, I prefer to have a quiet life, if possible, in private.'

Len Murray echoed his view: 'At heart I am a solitary person. Because of my background as a child I had few friends, and this led to a rather isolated existence.

'I have a few friends from the trade union movement at all levels, one of my closest friends is an ex-district officer, friends at the church—they're the more local ones—but then I'm happy to go to Burton-on-Trent for dinner—I've got lots of friends there, well, friends not in an intimate sense, but a good relationship.

'I'd as happily walk through Epping Forest by myself as with anybody else. I find it soothing, strips me of some of the self-concern, the feeling that if I stop running on the spot, the world will stop revolving on its axis.'

Lord Gormley also differentiates between being a loner and loneliness: 'I'm a loner in my own way. I like to get amongst people, but I don't like them to get inside me. I keep myself to myself. I know a lot of people personally, but yet I have very few personal friends.'

Often the sense of being alone determined direction at critical periods in the individual's career development. In the case of Lord Weinstock, it provided much of the impetus for his early academic success: 'I suppose I've always been a bit of a loner ever since I was a child. I've always indulged in solitary pursuits, music and reading in particular, and I have always had a very small number of good friends rather than a lot of superficial friendships.'

Lord Weinstock talked of the position of leadership being of necessity a solitary one, the message that came over was that 'the buck stops here', and it comes home to roost in a very personal way. 'I must regard everything we don't do well as a personal failure ... I am exposed to the world and to my own work people, and this is a constant and considerable pressure. Public confidence is the key to the success and impetus of any firm. If I don't do well then people lose confidence. I am responsible for everything. I can't shift the blame if we have a bad manager, it's my fault for putting him there.'

And yet Lord Weinstock doesn't seem completely comfortable in this, a totally isolated role. When asked about areas of stress in his life, they seemed paradoxically to revolve around loneliness, but a forced loneliness and not one of his own choosing. 'The worst moments I can remember are times of feeling isolated. When I went up to Cambridge I felt very much alone. My fellow students were better educated, much more self-assured and so I threw myself into my work. There was nothing else.'

We have found in other research that the experience of social isolation can determine direction at critical periods in the individual's career development. Enoch Powell, for example, saw it as providing much of the impetus for his early academic success. He too would see himself essentially as a loner. 'When I went to Cambridge I was out of my depth. I hadn't learned what else there was to do in life except to work and compete—so I worked and competed.' Powell highlights the essential paradox of the loner as he sees it: 'Yes, I am a loner by nature. Not that I don't have friends—I have good friends and I do enjoy working in a team setting such as a college or a regiment. But I have no sense of fear or anxiety if I find myself alone either physically or intellectually. I am a natural mountaineer.'

It seems that Lord Weinstock justifies his individualistic stance and sees it as a desirable strength for a man in his position. 'I have to be ruled by pragmatism. My *raison d'être* is to satisfy the customer and decisions have to be made to create maximum wealth. I must use logic to suppress my ego, otherwise it is impossible to be objective. I do not allow conversation to take place when we have to decide, all data must be collected and the logical decision will be taken.'

So he presents a picture of a rational decision-making style, rather cold and clinical in its execution. Here, perhaps, the strengths of the loner prove advantageous and can be seen psychologically as a measure of high self-actualisation.

However, at the same time as stressing the isolation of his role, he rather wistfully commented that: 'One of my greatest satisfactions is working with a few people who you can trust—and love. People who rely on you and on whom you can rely. This is, I suppose, true comradeship, and there is some joy in that!'

Sara Morrison regrets the loneliness she has experienced during her career. Although she sees it as an inevitable facet of the leadership role, it has been one which she has found particularly difficult to come to terms with as a woman. 'Leadership of any sort makes for a certain kind of solitariness ... Any individual will have only so much energy and personal resources, and (in my case) they have been spread very widely. So one is inclined to do what one has to do and be where one has to be. The rest of the time, as far as I am concerned, I tend to pull up the drawbridge in order that I can refuel the boilers. There are times when I need to get right away from the conflab of meeting the public or whatever.'

Sara Morrison went on to comment, 'You know, the isolated "star" is a very, very real syndrome. Even in my own small way I can understand that, and I can see how it happens. But it is sad when it does occur, and it is saddest of all for women because they are not so naturally gregarious as men.'

For Jonathan Miller too the loneliness is not of his own choosing. He attributes his feelings of loneliness to the success of his career: 'Many people look at me and say "You're famous, you make a lot of money, what an enviable life," and yet ... I visit the play *The Seagull* about every five years, and I've directed it three times, and each five years that I revisit it, the great long speech of Tregorian about what it's like being a famous writer strikes deeper and deeper wounds as I hear it. It seems to be more and more accurately a picture of the life that I've led.

'I feel lonely a lot of the time. It is the sort of loneliness that comes on you, partly as a result of being well known, because when you become well known several things happen to you. First, you obviously change your life—not because you move around with more famous people, that is the paranoid fantasy of those with whom you worked previously. They say "Oh, he wouldn't want to know us, he's spending his time with the Duchess of Devonshire and Paul Newman," and he's not! There are people who withdraw from you in the belief that I won't want to see them because they think that you'll think that they are too dull. Actually people pull away from you. If you were associated with professional academic people, they themselves are filled with all sorts of disdains for the theatre and there is something very interesting which gives it away. I think what gives it away is this: when I talk to, more occasionally now, some of my previous friends, ex-colleagues who are either in academic work or higher ranks of the Civil Service or in what one would call serious jobs or serious pursuits, they will talk about what I'm doing by saying, "What's it like being in showbiz?" but they talk about going to the theatre as a description of what they do. They visit the theatre, I work in showbiz. In other words, the participants of the theatre are exponents of showbiz. The clients of the theatre are consumers of art. So it is a very peculiar thing, the art as it is exhibited and as an experience, a serious thing, but the making of art is done by frivolous, silly people.'

So, overall, the members of our group seem to display a marked degree of psychological independence which is generalized by a 'loner' image. This is recognized by them, and indeed, is seen by all as a particular source of strength, though its negative aspects are also acknowledged.

Obviously because of their key positions, all of this group have to work very closely with a whole range of colleagues. In this it seems as if they are, in a sense, 'multilingual'. They can move easily and skilfully into different modes or styles as the circumstances dictate. However, fundamentally, they have one 'mother tongue' which is seen by them as an essential part of their 'core' self. They are, at heart, independent and 'loners'.

**THE OUTSIDER**

There seems to be a real advantage in being a cultural outsider in order fully to practise this independence. Sir Peter Parker highlights this point: 'I came as a refugee to this country in my early years. This was an enormous advantage to me as I was able totally to ignore the class system and to make my own way. It was a terrific advantage not to be carrying all that clobber. I got to Oxford by buying a map at the station and walking round knocking on doors. I had three places by the end of the day.'

When Sir Michael Edwardes was asked if it was difficult for him as a South African to move into a position of power in this country, he expressed the contrary view: 'In fact, I had a tremendous advantage because I was far more critical and outspoken of what I found here than local people seemed to be ... In fact, it must have been received quite well. I got to the board of my company when I was 39 and became chairman at 44. I suppose people thought my lack of tolerance and frustration with the situation was more than justified.'

Sara Morrison, on the other hand, feels that the British class system to a certain extent contributed to her feelings of isolation: 'I don't know that anybody fits in with anybody. I mean, I never did. It's not a case of not getting on with people, it's just that you don't connect with them in quite the same way, because you are different. And so you're a sort of oddity, at least in my case, coming from what would be labelled "privileged upper class background". In old-fashioned terms I think that's doubly isolating, there's not the sort of in-built meritocracy structure into which I automatically fit because I didn't come from the same structure.'

**CONCLUSION**

'Those who are too lazy to think for themselves and be their own judges obey the laws. Others sense their own laws within them; things are forbidden to them that every honourable man will do any day of the year, and other things are allowed to them that are generally despised. Each person must stand on his own feet.'

Herman Hesse in his book *Demian* sums up the essence of our successful 'change maker'.

He or she is independent and self-sufficient, secure in their inner selves and judgements. As indicated earlier, they 'march to the beat of their own private and inner drum'. They are not involved in the obsession of trying daily to prove themselves. As Fyodor Dostoevsky laments about men in general, in his *Letters from the Underground*, 'The whole work of man really seems to consist in nothing but proving to himself every minute that he is a man and not a piano-key'.

They are aided in their independence by being, on the whole, 'outsiders looking in'. We can see that many of them came from minority or boundary groups in society. This may have provided them with a more dispassionate view of mainstream activity, which now extends to business, trade union affairs, and management. Although they are not *dependent* on others, and may be able to reach more objective and less-distorted judgements, they tend to maintain *interdependent relationships* with work colleagues and *social support* from a close-knit family—as we will see later in the book.

# CHAPTER FOUR

# CAREER PATTERNS

*'It [work] is about a search, too, for daily meaning as well as daily bread, for recognition as well as cash, for astonishment rather than torpor; in short, for a sort of life rather than a Monday through Friday sort of dying. Perhaps immortality, too, is part of the quest.'*

Studs Terkel

Alistair Mant, in his book *The Rise and Fall of the British Manager*, suggests that executive success is frequently achieved by people from relatively humble origins. This was true of many of the members of the group we interviewed. Even those who came from a privileged background often felt deprived in terms of starting their career. As Lord Longford suggests: 'No, I wasn't born with a silver spoon, more of a bronze one I suppose. My brother inherited everything. I remember my mother calling me in and saying, "You must realize that you will never be able to afford to marry". I was very disadvantaged within my own family and setting ...'

## EARLY RESPONSIBILITY

It was quite surprising to us that many of our 'change makers' started their careers 'at the bottom', in fact often in very humble positions. Lord Gormley, recognized as one of the most successful

43

union negotiators of modern times, started this way. 'When I worked in the pits, of my own accord, I very rarely used the union, although I was always a member from being nearly 14, up to being the age of 30-odd. I was from the age of 17-18 on production schemes, I was either coal cutting, or ... I was always on the production end of it. Normally, working with a small group of workers (perhaps two or three), and funnily enough, it seemed to go that I became their leader. Sometimes it happens in society, there's a person accepted as leader, and other people are willing to be led by them. I always had this job, and I was then negotiating for that small group, and I would negotiate directly with the manager on behalf of that group. That's where I learned my negotiating.

'You were working under private owners in those days, before nationalization, and the colliery manager had a little more say in what you could do and what you couldn't do in any one given point of time, and therefore you could go and negotiate with him, and you would have to prove to him. I only went to the pit to earn money—all these songs about "I like working" are a load of codswallop! You go to work for money. And I was always in that position, to be getting more money for doing the same work as an individual and other men at my own colliery. Then when I became the leader of a group, I went to negotiate contracts that would give them a better return than other men doing similar work in the same pit. Then I negotiated the bloody contract. And when all the people would come to me, they'd say "What the hell? You don't know how to negotiate." And I'd say "That's up to you!" So then I was elected and became an active member of the union, more or less by accident than by anything else.'

Sir Michael Edwardes started his successful entrepreneurial career in his late teens launching a haulage/contracting business whilst he was still an undergraduate at Rhodes University. 'The risk was ours, the profit was ours. There I was, a student, with a tiny holiday business—the classic Capitalist.

'When I was 21 I joined Chloride and quite soon was put in to take over a small branch company that we had bought. All the way along in Chloride I was involved in recovery-type situations which implied change.'

A decade later, having risen rapidly through the ranks of the company and with a series of successes beneath his belt, he found himself at the age of 33 with a total remit to 'sort out Central Africa'. This he achieved through a bold programme of rationalization, which foreshadowed on a lesser scale many aspects of his later plans for the rescue of British Leyland.

Sarah Morrison pointed to a need to explore her own limits and the heady excitement of early success. 'I have told you before that I was an only child and somewhat of an individual. I think I was always stimulated by new and novel situations. I was always a sort of scholar just testing the system to see how much further one could go. I tended to walk through doors just to see what was on the other side. I wanted to be involved in whatever was going on, in whatever direction presented itself at the moment. It was entirely self-generated even that far back, and I guess it is still with me today. There was a certain stimulus about being the youngest to do everything. I was the youngest that had ever done this and the youngest that had ever done that. I can remember it had a certain sort of stimulus. I must admit that I still find it quite a shock when I realize that I am probably now the oldest!'

Arthur Scargill became a member of the National Executive of the Communist Party at the early age of 16. In that capacity he visited Moscow and whilst he was there met President Khruschev. At 17 he started work underground and within months had led his fellow apprentices out in direct opposition to union advice. He paid a price for this action and was expelled from the local branch, but the Yorkshire Area headquarters reversed the branch decision. He was reinstated and the conditions which led to the strike were improved. It was the first of a series of head-on conflicts he was to have with the establishment, both within the management and the union.

Clive Jenkins expressed some pride both in his decision to give up his scholarship at the local Grammar School to go into local industry and in the rapid success that followed. 'We didn't have much money, and I had a real itch to go to work as well as to study. At the time I had a cousin living in the same street who had gone into a new works in the town producing alloy sheeting for aircraft. She seemed to have a nice job. She worked in the Test

House and I remember she wore a white coat! After some persuasion she arranged for me to see the works manager. I was just fourteen.

'So off I went one Saturday morning, in my school blazer with red ribbons round it and my school-cap with the metal badge on it, to meet him. A man who I learned later was a byword in the industry ... I went off to work then at first as a labourer in the Test House and he paid for me to go to Swansea Technical College. So in between shifts I used to go off to do some studying. A bit risky at the time as they were bombing Swansea quite often! ...

'So I became a metallurgist ... I think I was the youngest person to enlist on the college's metallurgy course. This was very "up market" you see. There were great jobs in South Wales for metallurgists and sanitary inspectors! They were both thought to carry money, and most of all prestige!

'I qualified and I remember that everybody else was going off to the war and getting killed. I was just a bit too young to go. I tried to volunteer for the Navy but got into trouble when they found that I was in a reserved occupation. Anyway by the time I was 18, I was a Chief Chemist in a small laboratory. I was responsible for a team of eight or nine other people and I was being paid quite a lot of money ... I was doing very well indeed.

'In the meantime I had joined the Scientific Workers Union and had become both Branch Secretary and Unit Treasurer, all before I was turned 18! By the time I was 20 I became the youngest full-time trade union official ever to be appointed.'

If early responsibility is denied in one area then it seems the frustrated 'change maker' will search for an alternative field in which to express himself.

Jonathan Miller provides a vivid example of this. While following in his father's footsteps at medical school, Miller also became interested in the theatre. His first job was as a surgical houseman, and it was at that time that he was invited to participate in a revue for the Edinburgh Festival. He goes on to say: 'It was a sideline, a fortnight on holiday between two jobs and I was going to do it, but then this catastrophic recognition occurred. This was due to the fact that I had undergone some disappointment or apprehension about the professional prospects of medicine, as they were at the end of the fifties, when the ladder seemed to narrow very rapidly, immediately after qualification. It seemed unduly crowded and a very ugly sort of competitiveness entered into the appointments for Registrar jobs in the year or two immediately after qualification. I had seen around me lots of very disappointed, weary, tired and embittered Senior Registrars and Junior Registrars who were lining up 20 or 30 for one Junior Registrar job, often in very unattractive positions.

'I felt at that time that I would go into entertainment for the moment, make enough money so that when I was doing these terribly competitive jobs, I could afford to not be paid very much. One was paid very little money in those days.

'I think my parents were both very apprehensive about my switching. They didn't anticipate at that time that I was going to switch permanently, and I didn't myself.'

At this point an opening arose in medicine. Jonathan Miller turned this down as he was disappointed by the strong competition in the field, and also because of the extremely poor pay at the time. 'I had always had a fairly comfortable life, if not over prosperous, then at least a comfortable upper middle class professional world of nice books and so forth. The idea of me having to move every two years to poky digs and bring up children, perhaps in reduced circumstances, while fighting a rearguard action with other Registrars, seemed to me a rather ghastly sort of life to have to lead. I persuaded myself I could always go back to medicine. I persuaded myself even for four or five years that I could always go back—even to the extent of actually doing a job during the day while I was doing "Beyond the Fringe".'

John Harvey-Jones has been a 'two career' man, but not entirely through his own choice. He joined the Navy at the age of 12 and graduated from Dartmouth in time for the outbreak of World War Two.

'Of the two main influences on my life that I can discern [the other was his relationship with his parents] probably the greatest was the Navy. I learned such a lot that was to stand me in good stead. For instance, the Navy really did insist upon one thing. It insisted that you were not born to leadership. You had to earn the right to lead and the Navy was very, very clear on how those rights were earned. They had simple rules. If the chaps were working then you were bloody working too! When you came back on board ship you were the last guy to go and have your meal, small but important things. They stressed the importance of personal leadership, the importance of getting to know all your people. But above all the Royal Navy prided itself as being for an elite. It prided itself as being an organization which would only accept things which were as near perfection as it could get.'

It was an environment that moulded the young midshipman and one he found totally conducive to his nature. The Navy became both father and mother to him. He served her well, internalizing her high standards, standards which remain with him to this day.

'I felt a continuous need to prove myself ... I was sunk a couple of times on destroyers before I was 18. What did I do then? I felt I had to go and seek a more demanding role. So I volunteered for the submarine service. I joined and I stayed in submarines for the rest of the war. When the war ended I went and learned Russian and then I worked for the Intelligence Service for many years.'

Reluctantly he turned his back on the Navy when his daughter contracted polio, and started a new career in industry. 'When I left the Navy I came straight to ICI. Well actually I was unemployed for a while, having left on the understanding that I'd got a job in ICI. I must say it was quite a change! I started as a Work Study Surveyor, which is the lowest sort of grade. At that time they couldn't get any normal graduate, or anyone else for that matter, to do a Work Study job. It was pretty "yukky". In fact it was very instructive in many ways but it was still a pretty "yukky" job! So I started at the bottom here at Head Office and I have worked my way up!'

The opportunity to assume early responsibility seems an essential element in the successful career patterns of our 'change makers'. All stressed its importance to them on an individual level and several saw it as of crucial importance in management training.

Sir Michael Edwardes is a strong advocate for encouraging this early responsibility. He talks enthusiastically about his own early exploits and how much he learned, often through his mistakes, of people and business.

He feels we need to consider seriously 'the concept of creating space' in order to develop the new generation of managers currently joining commerce and industry. For without 'space' potential will be stifled, skills and abilities will atrophy. Space, he believes, will lead to real growth 'elbowing inertia, apathy and resistance to change aside'.

'Space' to Edwardes is early and genuine responsibility. It can and should be provided throughout British industry—'for where else is there such a challenge, where else are talents and resources so fully stretched. Where else do relatively young people have this "space" to grow and change?'

Sir Peter Parker echoes these sentiments exactly. He highlights the need to encourage new managers to 'sense their own scope'. The best training, he enthuses, is provided in the field where unrecognized potential can emerge directly from the demands of responsibility. 'Find training situations where they do find themselves "up the creek", sans paddle, sans corporate policy, sans corporate plan, and encourage them. Encourage them to trust their own judgement and encourage them to realize that this factor is there (lying dormant within). It is rather an exciting factor and it can make one hell of a difference.

'That is what maddens me about this country! Think of the war! El Alamein, if you credit it to Brigadier Williams, or whatever his name is now, he must have been in his late twenties! If you think of "the bastard enemy". Well Himmler was in charge at 33, and Heidrich was only about 27!

'In peace time we simply don't recognize how ready people are to take on responsibility—and how "stretchy" they really are.'

## STARTING FROM SCRATCH

You may find it difficult to believe that the cookery and restaurant entrepreneur, Prue Leith, should have started her business in such primitive beginnings as a bedsit in Earls Court. 'I had a bedsitter in Earls Court and I used to deliver food on the tube

49

(fruit flan on the Underground!), and also cooking in other people's houses. It was easy, because I didn't have to have any capital, because if I hadn't got the capital to get the ingredients together I would ask them to buy in, and have them on the kitchen table when I got there, or I would buy them on their account at Harrods, because I was cooking for rather rich ladies. Or they would advance me the money to go and buy the food and then I would cook it and they'd give me the money for cooking it. I'd charge five bob extra for washing up, or waiting at table, and gradually I got rather good at it!

'I also took a job when I left cookery school, with a firm of solicitors, doing just three days a week, and that paid £8 per week I remember, and as the rent was £4 per week it meant I didn't have to do a lot more work to live.

'One of the problems with people is that they eat at unsocial hours, I mean cooking's not a 9 to 5 job; people tend to eat on Christmas Day and in the evenings, and on Saturdays and Sundays particularly. And because I had no relatives in England, and I was living on my own, I never minded working weekends, I would cook anywhere that people would pay me to cook.

'I used to work at night a lot, because I would be writing a recipe book or whatever (making pâté for pubs all over the place at one time), and the only time my oven was free for such long slow cooking (because all day long I was cooking people's lunches and dinners, etc.) would be at night. Do you know I still can't eat liver terrine to this day? I used to make 50 lb of it at a time. Cook it in roasting tins in batches, and it took all night to cook, but I used to set the alarm to put top to bottom and turn them round; and if I was doing meringues for a wedding I would do them at night, and I'd have to run them over and turn them off and things, and I thought nothing of working all the way through the night! When I opened the restaurant I would quite often go to the market (all three—Covent Garden, Smithfield and the fish market), and get back to my catering company, do the morning work with them and deliver a few lunches to customers, come here to work, go home to sleep for a couple of hours, come here to work again until the restaurant closed, go home and sleep again. For a good two years I would sleep three hours and three hours (two bites of the cherry!), and the other nights I'd sleep seven or eight hours (the intermediate nights), and I got so used to it.'

Sir Michael Edwardes joined his first (and up to British Leyland, his only) company, Chloride, at the age of 21 as a management trainee. He was based in London, working at Gaedor, Chloride's motor parts subsidiary in Tottenham Court Road. Here he served on the trade counter and was a general factotum, sweeping out and delivering batteries to garages in the local area. He was eventually transferred to Dukinfield in Lancashire where he shared digs with six other people, the most exalted of whom was a trainee manager from Woolworths.

Edwardes returned to South Africa with Chloride's praises ringing in his ears. A few years later he was running Chloride in Salisbury.

Even those of the group who had the indirect advantage of higher education often found themselves in rather undramatic departments, doing lowly jobs.

Clare Mulholland obtained her first appointment through her university appointments office, attending a typical university jobs fair, and then subsequently an interview in London. 'I joined ICI as an indexer, which is where they took about a dozen women graduates a year then (it's a glorified filing clerk, but I was attached to the Personnel Department, with some kind of training brief, so I knew that there was a possibility of moving on, or so they claimed, if I learned "well"). I felt that as ICI was the largest company, and I knew absolutely nothing about industry, it couldn't be a waste of time, no matter how lowly it was, and how routine—that it was up to me to learn whatever I could from it. So I did that, and at the time I was with a number of other girls who had been taken on, who were very, very dissatisfied because they felt it was inferior work and so on. It sounds very pious to say that, but I don't mean it in a pious way at all. I thought that their expectations—just because they were graduates, they had something to contribute—were pretentious. So after a year, when I'd begun to think "I hope something else might be coming along within ICI", there was a vacancy in the Public Relations Department. I knew absolutely nothing about public relations, but it seemed to me that somehow I might, because I looked up the internal staff directory and it had "Film Department" and "Advertising", and I suddenly thought "Maybe that would be quite interesting". So I joined them, and I think that probably was really the luckiest break I had, because I joined a very, very good professional department of delightful people (most of them ex-journalists), terrific fun, but very, very good.

'I learned then a great deal, I think, about how to deal professionally. The other thing about them was, although there was a hierarchy of rank, they were very unhierarchical. As if there were about six of us (as press officers), you can imagine the range of calls you get with a company like ICI—it can be anything from dyslexia or the *Investor's Chronicle* or *Woman* magazine, that were all kinds of things to do with the company and its wide trading. And so a call from anybody might just come through to you, even though you were the most junior—then it was up to you to know how to deal with it, and so that was very, very good training, as well as a happy atmosphere and fun and so on.'

Although Jeremy Isaacs had the obvious advantages of an Oxford education, his career beginnings were also tentative. 'Somebody gave me the names of people in television to write to, and I applied for a job in Granada. There was no job advertised, but I asked Granada had they anything for me. And I applied for a job at the *Observer*, which was advertised, which I didn't get. I had written very little at Oxford (something, but not very much), mostly it had been speech-making, chairing committees, talking, arguing, making jokes, very verbal I was in those days—far more so than now—but I decided to try and be a journalist.

'I don't know if somebody advised me to do it, or I decided to do it, but I decided the best way to try to crack this magic circle was to demonstrate what I could do, so I wrote articles, which I didn't get paid for, and begged people to take them for *Tribune* and *Forward* (two Labour weeklies of the time). I sent them of course to other places, but they wouldn't publish them. I remember I did get something published in the *Glasgow Herald*, and so eventually when the chap at Granada was going to give me a job, I obviously wasn't just what he thought I was when I came through the door (spare Oxford graduate). But I had actually written an article about the 1958 bus strike in London, and I'd gone to see a busman, and he'd introduced me to his wife, and she'd gone through her family weekly budget, where her husband's wage went, and on the basis of that, and the sort of impression I'd made talking to the two or three people who'd seen me before this chap saw me, I was hired by Granada Television. I had to go and live in Manchester. I was hired as a researcher, which is the equivalent of a junior reporter, for news and current affairs.

'And, because I had abilities that were not being called into play very adequately on the daily, and the absolutely droolingly trivial weekday current affairs programme that they did, and one or two people obviously had their eye on me, within 15 months I was given an opportunity. First of all I organized a major piece of political television for them—a thing called "Marathon", which they did during the General Election of 1959, when they invited every single candidate in the Granada area to use television to address the electorate, which was laborious, but ... And then they really gave me opportunities to produce and I realized that I had been lucky.'

Mary Quant had already decided on the career she would follow at a very early age. 'I inherited clothes as a small child but they were not my style. I started trying to make my own clothes at 6 and 7. It was ridiculous. And then I spotted my style in one child at dancing classes. It summed it up. It was everything I had always wanted to look like and be. She had a "Vidal" haircut. She did tap dancing and not ballet classes. She wore a long black sweater, a three-inch-long black skirt, black tights and black patent leather shoes with a button on the top and white socks. It was so chic— it was just it!

'I remember trying to make these clothes from the rather rigid clothes, ones you have to behave in, which came from my cousin. So I really wanted to make clothes from then on, but for myself really.

'So then I wanted to go to a fashion school to do this but my parents and teachers so rightly decided that the fashion business was too risky. They were advanced in that they thought that it was important equally for boys and girls to have a career. So I went to a straight art school where you could learn to be an art teacher. I went to Goldsmiths, where I met Alexander [her husband], who was also there. I had longed actually to go to St

Martin's, or one of those. In retrospect I can see that I was terribly fortunate because in the fashion schools then you were taught and taken to Paris to see the collections, which you then mangled out into something which was mass-producible but exactly the same look and all the rest of it. They were designing clothes for women who went to balls and who barely wore day clothes at all, certainly didn't have a job. And so there was no relationship between what people wore and hence this very artificial style of clothes and very rigid beehive hair—a denial of any possibility of work, and that's what people who did go to work had to wear.'

Her husband, Alexander Plunkett-Greene, reflecting on their early days, commented, 'Ours is a very special case. Being my age, I remember very clearly the War itself and the way it extended in terms of the way it affected social life for seven or eight years after. People like me grew up in very dreary times and at the same time it was when people, young people, started having economic and moral freedom, and later power. There was also a great swing to Socialism, and the young suddenly found themselves not being told by their parents' generation, because their parents' generation knew that they had got it wrong before.

'If you could afford to, you could go to the cinema; you couldn't afford to go to restaurants for decent food. But you could go in and buy yourself some egg and chips. The decision was, do I buy ten cigarettes and go to the cinema or have egg and chips? The cinema was terrible, the food was terrible, there was no music except old-fashioned jazz. Then the Teddy Boys came along, looking like new people, and then the first coffee bars started—in pubs you could only really drink beer, and they were very manly and squalid places. These coffee bars were terrific and then we thought, "Why don't we try and do a restaurant?" Then we thought, "Why don't we do a shop?" because clothes were wrong and we must try and get clothes right. Art students like us thought that we were an elite group. This was the time when Tommy Steele appeared in his outrageous clothes. Revolution was in the air and we started a restaurant where impecunious people could eat cheap, but reasonably good food, and were waited on by waiters in tight trousers who called you "dear". We made clothes for art students like us, but which actually expressed "The Look".'

## THE LADIES' HANDICAP

*'Even when the path is nominally open—when there is nothing to prevent a woman from being a doctor, a lawyer, a civil servant—there are many phantoms and obstacles, I believe, looming in her way.'*

Virginia Woolf

It seems as if the career beginnings of senior women executives, in one way or another, are adversely affected by the very fact that they are *women*. As the United Nations report in 1980 indicated, 'Women constitute *half* the world's population, perform nearly *two thirds* of its work hours, receive *one tenth* of the world's income, and own less than *one hundredth* of the world's property.' What this of course means for any woman trying to achieve a senior role in industry is that the 'going is going to be rough'. It is not surprising, however, that women constitute between 15 and 25 per cent of all managers in most Western developed countries. According to the International Labour Office *Year Book of Labour Statistics*, published at the beginning of 1980, in the US, with the strongest legislation affecting the employment of women, only 24 per cent of managers and administrators are women, followed by the UK at 18.8 per cent. Even so, in the UK, the occupations in which women are likely to be managers are traditionally female occupations such as retailing, catering and personnel. In this respect, once again the US situation is somewhat better. For example, in 1979 there were 300 women on the boards of the 13 largest companies in the US, an improvement from 147 women in 1976. However, in Britain, of the top UK companies, only two had women directors in 1979.

Our sample of women executives highlight the difficulties that women face. Prue Leith feels that the male top manager's attitude towards women is that they are 'gentle and meek and lacking aggression'. So what, asks Prue: 'I'm on the Board of British Rail; one of only around 20 women, there are hardly any women in BR management! Nearly all of them are graduates who came in on the management training scheme, and the only reason they've been allowed in at all is because the law won't let the men discriminate. But they say when they're given a job after the training, and they get put in an area manager's office or something, that the worst discrimination is not the over-straight hatred, which they get from many of the old-fashioned BR managers who say things like "Well, I'm having a woman over my dead body in this office", and "It's a man's job", because they know that they can beat that by being good at their job and overcoming it. But what they find very hard is this avuncular, patronizing nice guy who says things like, "It's not a woman's job really, I'll go and talk to the men about their rostering, you sit here and type letters". They find it very difficult, because they're trained (like all women) to be gentle, and meek, and it's difficult for them to say, "Tough luck, I'll go and talk to the men about the rostering—you do the typing!"

'There is an absolutely fascinating report on women in conversation. Some guy went around measuring how much women talked and how much men talked, and in mixed company women don't talk at all! If you go to a cocktail party, the man talks and the woman encourages, she does the interviewer technique, and if women talk, men raise their voices and come in and shut them out. It's interesting, because one of the things I noticed at BR is that a lot of the women, say most of the women managers, manage in a less aggressive style than men. They don't believe in confrontation and they try to sort things out and talk to people, and they behave more like mothers. And the man writing the reports on these women each year, and seeing them at interview, etc., very frequently says to them, "You must develop more aggression, you must be stronger". And the women want to say, "Stop telling me how to do it, just judge me by results! Do you mean that I'm not getting the men to work on time—am I failing?" And the men say, "Oh no, the results are fine, but you'll never get on if you can't be more aggressive". Well, that's a totally male idea of management, it's unnecessary—there are many male managers who manage in a quiet, unconfronting, gentle manner, and no one questions them!'

Clare Mulholland, on the other hand, feels that more women executives need role models to enhance their career. At the moment, she suggests, married women with children are at a great disadvantage in the promotion stakes in British industry. 'I do believe, genuinely, that I've been lucky in that before I've ever found a job frustrating, or limiting, there seems to have been another opportunity open to me. But I have to say that I think it's been easier for me to move around or to move up as a woman because I'm single and have no children. I have no doubt that if I were married, and especially if I had children, I could not have had the same career pattern, because domestic factors would have intervened. And I think that for most men, I know that men sometimes have the problems of working wives, and not disturbing their career pattern, but on the whole I still think the pattern is for a couple or a family to follow a man's career. So I think that's the greatest difficulty that women have, and I observe women and discuss things a lot, because I'm very interested in the position of women in broadcasting and other industries. I'm still disappointed that it still seems such a rarity to find women at or near the top at management at any level, but I think it just can't be done overnight. Too many women still lack confidence to put themselves forward. I think it is a question of confidence, and I don't mean (I hope), that I'm over-confident. But I was struck when I heard somebody say somewhere that successful women often put their success down to luck, and very few men do, and he said that's because women simply always play themselves down. Well, maybe that's so, but if it's just a question of saying, although I believe it's also luck, I'd rather have that than overbearing arrogance! But I think it's a pity that women often need encouragement and I must have been lucky in the men I have worked for, because I have never worked for women. So the men I've worked for, I feel, have never given me the impression that I couldn't do something, because I was a woman, or I couldn't advance. Along the way, of course, you get some patronizing, and some put-downs, but then so does everybody.

'I think women do understand the domestic pressures on all women whether married or single or whatever, and are perhaps more accommodating of that, so that it can be quite jolly to work together with other women. I would certainly, and have always in the last few years, as I've moved up a bit, felt a great deal of responsibility for encouraging younger women to feel that it is possible to move up, and to understand how they have to tackle things. So I feel that (it sounds a bit like a Sunday School teacher) one ought to offer encouragement, and always be willing to advise, because I think it's very, very important that women who are in senior positions are accessible as role models to other younger women to understand that they too can make it. But I would never say that jobs should be given to women just to make up numbers of quotas, and I have to say, *believe*, that women get jobs probably because they're better than ... I mean, they have to be slightly better than men candidates—I still think that that's true.'

Sara Morrison reinforces this view that women perhaps miss out on the climb to the top, because they lack the role models, and consequently often have little idea of how to go about the search for success. 'Looking back and having thought about it in great detail, I wonder—why not more women? It's an interesting question—why aren't more women doing whatever? And when one thinks it through, I don't have any particular new insight, except that on the whole women don't want to, and don't know how to set about things even if they do want to, because they often get to the top by accident rather than on purpose, because they're women. I get the impression that it's much more difficult for professionally qualified women, to stop being feminist.

'In nine times out of ten, women subconsciously are the ones who give way or sublimate something that they want to do, to that which fits in with their social and home life.'

Often, because of this lack of direction, Sara Morrison feels they simply mirror the behaviour of the successful male executive. In her eyes a course of action which further disadvantages the aspiring female. 'Those women executives who isolate themselves from other women, simply because they are working to different schedules and with different responsibilities, tend to forget that they don't actually become a man! Their life style doesn't lend itself to that. In all probability they will still have to go home and wash up, and take the responsibility of the domestic scene. In that way women are doubly disadvantaged in the business world ... My generation of women have handled this badly, so that people like me look like over-motivated, hyperactive, over-assertive, "bulls" of our generation.'

It is obvious that the career development of highly motivated business women can be adversely affected by the attitudes of their male colleagues and bosses. However, women may also be blocked by other senior women—in fact, it may be easier for their careers if women were managed by a certain type of male executive. Elizabeth MacDonald raised these issues: 'At the time I was working in market research it was unusual to have many women executives, so all the people I was working with most of the time were men. You must remember there are all sorts of prejudices against men too. Prejudices against short men, prejudices against men who are Jewish, prejudices against men who are not Jewish. So you could list a lot of prejudices that men have to face. But, certainly, there are individuals who when they are recruiting are definitely antagonistic towards women. I think those people who have a tendency to be incompetent feel much more threatened by a woman than by a man. So some of the resentment that is directed our way is because of this exposure of incompetence. Because, let's face it, those women who do get on tend to be just that bit better than the equivalent male. So we have an edge because as a woman at a given management level we can assume we pose more of a threat to someone who is a bit inadequate. In fact you could say that in business there are a number of very definite advantages in being female. Because, just think, during all of my business career I have been dealing with men and very few women, and that is still the case. I have had so much more experience dealing with them than they have had dealing with me! This can give me a very real advantage! If, for example, I was reporting to a female director, I would have to think much more carefully about managing her than I would about reporting to a male director, simply because I have not had the same amount of experience. Similarly I have made more errors about recruiting female executives than I have about recruiting males, because I have not had so much experience of recruiting females.

'So I do think that there are some very real advantages in being a woman in business. Personally, I don't think that prejudice against women is something to get too hung-up about because it is relatively easy to overcome these difficulties. However, there will be times when the situation is impossible. If you are in a company

59

and they won't give you a satisfactory answer as to why you were not promoted or whatever, then the only alternative is to leave that company if you wish to develop your career. Certainly I would if I was confronted by that sort of thing. It would be their loss not mine!

'I think most men, if they are honest, have a very ambivalent attitude towards females' careers—they think it is a marvellous idea provided it doesn't affect their convenience personally. So you have to do quite a bit of negotiating and make up your mind about the things that matter personally to you.'

It seems, therefore, that the early career beginnings of most of our female 'change makers' was tempered and affected by the very nature of their gender. Even some of the male 'change makers' noted the importance of the wife's role in maintaining their career. Women are not only blocked in business terms, but also have to endure the work pressures of their husbands if they remain in the home. As Jeremy Isaacs illustrates: 'It certainly caused trouble for my wife, but I think she appreciates it. I also think that women today understand in ways they were not articulating 20 years ago what a terrible burden they are actually being asked to carry, if that is allowed to prevail. It's all very well understanding it, but should one tolerate it? She has had to tolerate it, and she should *not* have had to tolerate it to quite the same degree she has.'

## CONCLUSION

When we look at how the members of our group 'reached the top', we see a remarkably similar pattern to their career development. Many of them started from relatively humble or lowly beginnings, and then literally worked through the system. And they found, as Hegel, that 'experience must run counter to expectation if it is to deserve the name experience'. They were fortunate enough to have experienced early responsibility, which provided them with the opportunity for success or failure, development or stagnation. These opportunities were used to develop their entrepreneurial abilities in the reality of the workplace. It was a proving ground for the apprentice journeyman. Most importantly, though, they all had some degree of early success, success which often led directly to public or organizational recognition. This led to a career progression which must have made them feel like Dorothy (from the *Wizard of Oz*), who on entering Oz, remarked 'Toto, I have a feeling we're not in Kansas anymore ...' It might be suggested that many of these people were 'in the right place at the right time', but they also seemed to understand the past and future of their organization. They were able to live in St Augustine's three social time zones: 'There are only three times. A present of things past; a present of things present; and a present of things future'.

As far as the women were concerned, they seemed to suffer some career handicaps. This was partly due to the male-dominated organizations they began in (in terms of senior management), and also the 20th century dilemma facing all working women, the 'dual career family' and consequently the 'dual role' imposed on women in executive positions. Nevertheless, they were able to turn negative or blocking experiences into positive outcomes—a characteristic that best sums up all our 'change makers', male and female alike.

# CHAPTER FIVE

# PRIVATE LIFE

*'Mental health is not so much a freedom from specific frustrations as it is an overall balanced relationship to the world, which permits a person to maintain a realistic, positive belief in himself and his purposeful activities. Insofar as his entire job and life situation facilitate and support such feelings of adequacy, inner security, and meaningfulness of his existence, it can be presumed that his mental health will tend to be good. What is important in a negative way is not any single characteristic of his situation but everything that deprives the person of purpose and zest, that leaves him with negative feelings about himself, with anxieties, tensions, a sense of lostness, emptiness, and futility.'*

Kornhauser

Most companies expect a high level of commitment from their executives, in terms of, for example, long hours, frequent business trips and social entertaining. This can have beneficial effects on a manager's career, but at a cost. Indeed, Joseph Heller, in his book *Something Happened*, highlights this phenomenon in terms of his organizational Happiness Charts: 'At the very top [of the Happiness Charts], of course, are those people, mostly young and without dependants, to whom the company is not yet an institution of any sacred merit (or even an institution especially worth preserving) but still only a place to work, and who regard their present association with it as something temporary. To them, it's all just a job, from president to porter, and pretty much the same job at that ... Near the bottom of my Happiness Charts I put those people who are striving so hard to get to the top.'

We found in our assessment of the 'change makers' that the majority of them may have worked long hours that intruded into family life early in their careers, but when they achieved a certain amount of seniority or success, they tried to compartmentalize their work and family life. John Harvey-Jones expresses this succinctly: 'I live miles away from my work, because I happen to like living in the country and my family like living in the country. If anybody rings me up at home on business I go bananas! I mean, that's family time! I know all sorts of workaholics to whom it's a sort of silent machismo to ring up on a bloody Sunday. If anybody rings me up on a Sunday, I say "Look, I'm very sorry, I don't wish to be rude, is there something that only I can do?" And they generally say no, but if they say "Yes, I'm afraid it is", then I say "Well is it something that only I can do in the next 12 hours?" If they say no, I say "In that case, I'm sorry, I don't want to hear any more, you can ring me tomorrow morning at 8".'

This also applies to women who succeed in business, as Prue Leith illustrates: 'Well, the weekends are sacred. I don't care what it is, I wouldn't go to dinner at Buckingham Palace on Saturday night! I just wouldn't. I have very occasionally broken the rule on Friday nights, and I know there's one Friday night this year when I've just got to go and talk at a farmers' organization because I'm on a Quango which tries to encourage the marketing of good British produce. And this group have asked me to speak for four years running and for four years I've said no, I won't do it, and I've got such a guilty conscience about it that I've just given in. But I'm cross with myself for giving in, I think I should have said no, Friday nights are part of my weekend. So I'm religious about that, and I feel very badly if I'm writing a book or a speech or working on something and it's in my head the whole time at the weekend. Perhaps the children have gone swimming or something, and I'll sit at my desk for an hour or two, but I don't feel good about it, I think I'd rather be pruning the roses. I'm quite good at it. The interesting thing is once you've said "I don't work at weekends", it's much easier.'

Sara Morrison also prefers to keep her home life completely separate from her work life. When asked about her leisure pursuits, she talked about the need to find the space and the time to 'recharge her batteries', and to just 'sink into inactivity'.

'I have always had a lot of outside interests but they have always been related to some end result. I've always done everything for a reason, for an end product. So I don't paint badly on a Saturday afternoon in a corner. I've never been one for those sort of leisure activities. On the whole it is crucial for me to have my weekends free. And I just stop! I am a very good "do nothing" person. In fact doing nothing is one of my specialities! I can waste hours doing nothing, which includes having both the television and radio on at the same time and listening to neither. That's what I mean by doing nothing, and I can do it for enormous lengths of time!'

And similarly, Elizabeth MacDonald tries to draw a distinct line between her work and private life, whenever possible. 'Well, I don't think that anyone in a senior position works from nine to five, but there are times when one has to start very early or go in over the weekend. In general, at a certain stage in my career I tried to make a rule that if I had to do extra work, I would do it at the office and not take it home. You can sit over work for so long at home, whereas if you have had to go in early, like at six or seven o'clock to do it, it can concentrate the mind wonderfully. So I try not to do extra work at home as a general rule. It would be a real emergency if I was doing it.'

## SUFFERING SPOUSES

Even though most of the members of our group felt that it was important to differentiate their private from their public lives, most acknowledge that their spouses and children suffered. Jeremy Isaacs felt that his wife has had to 'put up' with his success and exposure. He continues: 'But the pressures are colossal, partly because of work. *The World at War* [series] was a three-year, seven-day-week stint. Partly because of the absence at work, one's absorption in work, and then partly (it didn't seem to matter in the early days, but may have mattered in ways that I didn't know or didn't then perceive), the fact that one was a tiny bit in the public eye. I think when I was making a reputation the kids were too young to be aware of any of that. But more recently because of the launch of Channel 4, I was not out of the newspapers and public eye for something like 15 months. The 15 months that surrounded the launch of the channel were horrendous! It seemed we were unable to pick up a newspaper without seeing some attack on me, or the channel, or whatever.'

Throughout his long leadership role in the TUC, Len Murray has strived to protect his family: 'I make a very definite distinction between my public life and my private life, and I am a very private person and very defensive of my family in terms of exposure to publicity and so forth.'

John Harvey-Jones is exceedingly sensitive to the potential impact of his career on his 'long suffering wife'. 'I think my wife has suffered a great deal for the cause. I'm conscious of that, and because of it, for example, I have never worked at home, never opened a book at home, it would be rude of me to do so. Because of it I religiously take off her birthday (my wife's birthday), my daughter's birthday, our wedding anniversary—I take off.'

He continued: 'On the subject of my family I have one absolutely rigid rule which I have never broken (oh, I think there was one time when I was on the border!). I never invite anyone to our home whom I do not consider to be a friend. I will not have acquaintances from work or entertain business people. Even if I am doing the biggest deal imaginable I will not have, in my home, somebody who is not a friend.'

John Harvey-Jones goes on to say that although he is prepared to give as much of himself as possible during working hours, his wife and family should not be used as an appendage to his business life. 'The problem has been that my wife married a naval officer. I mean, the naval life was hell for a marriage, but she doesn't like business. She's not interested in business ... and the things that go with the jobs that others derive so much pleasure from (I mean we get invited to the Prime Minister's house, and we could be out every night at the opera, and every single evening), but that is not what switches my wife on. Now, she has a certain number of them [duties] she just has to do, and I protect like hell—she doesn't like flying, so again, I don't see why she should fly. The company hires me; I give it everything I can give it. I don't consider they get my wife "thrown in" as a sort of bonus. So we do try to lead our own life, we have our values. We're not interested in the visible "Pomp and Circumstance". I like to carry my own bags, I hate guys to open doors for me. I loathe sycophancy.'

The same thing applies to the husbands of successful women. Prue Leith can quite clearly see the impact of her career and business on her husband: 'My husband's a great believer in women working. He doesn't have a specific job, he helps me here. He does all the accounts—he's very good at that. He's a writer—so he's more at home than I am, and he prefers it. I'm very gregarious and like social things, and he can't stand it. His idea of purgatory is a party! So, sometimes I lean on him and say, "Well you're coming!" But far more often I go by myself, because he doesn't want it, and I don't see why he should go when he doesn't like it—so I see a lot of people that he doesn't. It works very well.'

Many of the group tried to minimize the involvement of their spouses in their own careers, feeling that the indirect influence may have a sufficiently negative effect. Jeremy Isaacs commented: 'My wife's involved to an absolutely minimal extent. She's now got to the part where she'd probably like to be involved a bit more than I'll allow her to be. However, I have really kept them as separate as I possibly could.'

On the other hand, a couple of the group felt that, given the nature of their particular rôle, it was inevitable that family life would be intruded upon. Jonathan Miller makes the point that his work, because of its nature, often intrudes into his home life, and it is interesting to note that he feels that this has drawn the family together more. 'There have been periods when I have been away from home for six to eight weeks at a time, twice in one year, which I suppose has thrown some strain on my wife left at home to look after the children. But otherwise my life has been conducted very much at home. The life of a director very much throws his house open to a lot of his workmates and colleagues. They come into the house, your designers come in with models and things, actors come in to discuss things, you even have little "read throughs" of things. My children have in the past, when they were younger, been to many of the rehearsals. When I was working at Glyndebourne they sat through the whole of the opera and learnt it off by heart. In some strange way, though it is often thought that someone who works in the way that I work throws over family life, in some strange ways we have actually got it together more.

'There are conflicts only when I am overworked and anxious about things not going well. It is then really that the strain gets thrown upon them. I think it is very acute when it does get thrown on the family—the strain of depression and disappointment, of feeling that it is all worthless. Then I think I become quite a burden to my family!'

Arthur Scargill, on the other hand, feels that anything he does in private that adversely affects his public role, should be open to scrutiny, but that his domestic life should be private and protected. 'I think that one's private life is clearly defined and divided from public life—apart from if it impinges. Now if I was in a position where something I was doing in private was having an effect, for example, with bribery and corruption, on my public life, then I think that that is a proper area for saying that that is something that should be regarded as public as well as private. But I think it's a private life, whether you're married, or whatever you're doing, if you've ten mistresses, or whatever the hell you're doing, if it only matters to you—it's nothing to do with anyone else. Provided it doesn't affect in any way your public ability to do the job or create paintings or music or whatever.'

Lord Gormley, when he was President of the NUM, felt that he did not have a private life, that he should expect his family life to be open to public view. 'I don't have any private life. You're in the public eye all the time, it's like living in a glass ball. For a while it became irksome, now it doesn't worry me—it worries my wife a lot more than me, but again, not as much as it used to do. That's one of the costs that you gladly give up, the fact that your private life is non-existent, and everything you say, you have to say in a guarded way, because it's so often misinterpreted. I was speaking at a conference last week, and I happened to mention the fact that political pressure at the beginning of the year had had results. I'd said how surprising it was that pressure, if it's applied successfully and in a proper way, can get you results. I just languidly said "It's like pressing your wife, and hugging your wife, if you do it in a nice way then you'll get things done for you, whereas if you go at it like a bull at a gate you're likely to get a bloody thump!" And of course the press picked that up and said that I'd likened that to Maggie, which was never the intention—that's what the press do, they manipulate anything you say. You've got to be very careful on that! But other than that, as I say, you've got to foresake those things when you get in the capital end of this job, because I'd never any great ambition to be President of the NUM, all I wanted was to do my job, at whatever level I was chosen to do it, and as I say, I was put into the job, and I try to damn well do it!'

A few were lucky in that they have spouses who feel that they should be working and encourage them—particularly some of the women executives. We have already seen that Prue Leith received her husband's encouragement and support, and similarly, for Elizabeth MacDonald: 'My husband prefers me to work. He married somebody with a successful career and that is what he prefers.'

## SUFFERING CHILDREN

In a number of cases, our 'change makers' accepted responsibility for the effects of their careers on their children. Clive Jenkins stoically reflects: 'It means you're wrapping yourself into a quiet cocoon in order to work. Yes, I think it makes you a much worse parent, I'm sure—I have no doubt about that, because you do tend to retreat into yourself.'

Or sometimes, the children of successful people learn to cope with their parent's fame and constant exposure to publicity, as Jonathan Miller highlights. 'My children are sometimes a little bit put down by my success, my versatility, and it worries me. They are very good about me being well known, they are uninterested in it, they don't show off. It doesn't impress them because they know me and they know it causes me pain and therefore it doesn't seem to be a particularly valuable commodity.'

On the other hand, some of those we interviewed, particularly one or two women, adapted their careers to meet the needs of the children, as Elizabeth MacDonald illustrates: 'I would say that the impact of having a family as opposed to being unmarried is that they take up resource, and it is undeniably demanding, one couldn't pretend otherwise, but I think that it is worth trying to use one's skills and talents. They are a gift in life and I find it very difficult not working full-time, but I felt with all the house moves and so on that the children needed me to get them properly settled and I have worked part-time only. But now they have been at school since they were both four and a half, a school where they are both very happy, and my working full-time effectively means that I see them two hours less a day during the week.'

It is not, however, only the women who had adapted their careers to meet family needs, as John Harvey-Jones illustrates. He was an officer in the Royal Navy and would have continued that career, except for the fact that his daughter contracted polio. As the Navy required him to be highly mobile, which meant that he spent long periods of time away from his family, he left the Navy to spend more time with his daughter. 'When my daughter was born I left home at six weeks and didn't see her again until she was three.' As it happens, unselfishly meeting family needs is not always a constraint on one's ultimate career progress!

## THE FAMILY: THE BACKBONE OF SOCIAL SUPPORT

In almost all cases for the successful entrepreneurs, executives and trade union leaders, we noted that the family was the ultimate social support team. Like the well-developed belief system we dealt with in Chapter 2, it provided both men and women with the perspective to put the business world into proper context. As Jeremy Isaacs commented: 'I think that I got married before I got a job. I rang my parents and said I'd got some good news, and they thought it was a job, but I'd decided to get married. I married a nice Jewish girl, who had the added attraction to me of coming from a long way away. She came from South Africa, and she was a friend of a friend. We're still married, and happily married, and she has been an enormous prop and support to me throughout, and, indeed, I think it's absolutely crucial.'

Jeremy Isaacs again: 'The worst thing has been the eating into one's family life, but again it's very much a work ... I think I'm more relaxed about work, and I very much enjoy not working occasionally (for limited periods), but there is no doubt that the social obligations of this job and the way in which the hours of programme making stretch on into the evening. I used to think it was wonderful that I didn't have to get up in the morning and be at work before 10 or 10.30, but the consequence at the other end for a wife who had been sat at home all day, or is sometimes out working, hearing me ring up and say I'm not going to be home until 7 or 8, or it'll be nearer 9, and then not turning up until 10— that is dreadful!'

In fact, many of these well-known and successful personalities feel that the family life itself adds a new dimension to the business persona. Sir Peter Parker, talking of the relationship between work and family, sums up the feelings of many of the executives in the group. 'I think it is very important. It ought to be close in my view, because you need enormous support. God knows what sort of man I'd have been if my wife had left me or that relationship had cracked. The family to me is of enormous significance. I tend to watch very carefully the family relationships, because I know when the strains come, they're going to be needed, and a chap who's got a solid base is twice the man.'

He stressed how important the support of his family has been in times of difficulty and how fortunate he had been to have them around him when he needed them. 'My star has danced the whole time in these matters, but I do know the enormous importance of keeping the family vision onto the job. They offered me the British Rail job in '67, and I had a terrible time there, because I had no public reputation at the time, and it was the papers interpreting me as wanting more money and that kind of thing. And yet my stand was a certain one and I remember being able to talk it over with my family and my kids, and saying "Well look, it isn't going to be good, but this is the stand".'

Richard Ingrams sees the family in general and children in particular as providing sanity and security in what at times can seem a mad existence. 'I think that people who don't have children miss out on that. Often you see people of my age at this time of life who are cracking up and they tend to be people who have no children. They don't have that support.'

## CONCLUSION

Although 'work at least gives him a secure place in a portion of reality in the human community', as Freud wrote in *Civilisation and Its Discontents*, the members of our group seemed haunted by the effect that work and success would have on their private life and families. By its very nature, high level and demanding work must inevitably spill over into domestic and family life. The potential cost of this was well recognized by each person we interviewed and almost all had well-developed strategies to protect the family from the threat and pressures of their work. However highly committed and motivated they were in their respective jobs, our group imposed very real limitations on the extent to which their family would be allowed to be involved. Indeed, the wife/husband and children become 'no go' areas to be defended, in most cases, at all costs. But most important of all, all the change agents recognized the importance of their family as their 'social support team', the ultimate support network to individuals who are self-confessed loners.

# CHAPTER SIX

# CHANGE

*'It should be borne in mind that there is nothing more difficult to arrange, more doubtful of success, and more dangerous to carry through than initiating changes ... The innovator makes enemies of all those who prospered under the old order, and only lukewarm support is forthcoming from those who would prosper under the new.'*

Niccolò Machiavelli

The former Chairman of BL holds that change, its implementation and control, must be of central concern in any developing society. Sir Michael Edwardes clearly sees himself as a 'change maker' and considers that instigating and directing change is *the* cornerstone of the managerial function. Indeed, he feels that response to change is central to most human endeavours. In his speech to Rhodes University in 1980 on the occasion of his acceptance of an honorary doctorate in law, he commented, 'If I have reached any conclusion from my experiences so far it is this: if there is a touchstone to human attitudes, that touchstone is change. How nations, how business, how men and women come to terms with change is a measurement of themselves.'

## 'GREAT MAN' VERSUS 'ENVIRONMENTALIST'

There are two historical schools of thought about the nature of change and 'change makers' or leaders. There are those who feel that the characteristics of the individual determine leadership (the 'great man' approach), and there are those who feel that the situation or circumstance at the time dictates the leader (the 'environmentalist' approach). We noted this division of thought among the group we interviewed.

Although Sir Peter Parker feels that the environment plays a role in business leadership, he also feels that the natural instinct predominates: 'I think I went to university just to get a degree to equip me slightly better to go into business, which I had in mind anyway. I mean, I've got an entrepreneurial instinct, I understand about making money and buying and selling—not that I've made money for myself really.'

Sir Michael Edwardes would agree. 'I think it's partly environmental, because I grew up in a business family, and partly natural instinct (probably way back in my Welsh ancestry).

'I think there's quite a lot of instinct about it. I don't think you could train a very bureaucratic animal to have a business instinct. It is an instinct because I don't think you can inculcate it into somebody very easily. Jewish people are born with it. The evidence is there; they're very good at it. I think at the end of the day it's a fundamental understanding of economics really. It's a "seat of the pants" approach to it. I don't think that your very effective, small-time Jewish trader thinks of it in economic terms. It's a "seat of the pants" approach to the fundamental laws of economics, which the average person in this country, funnily enough, hasn't got.'

Although Lord Gormley, former President of the NUM, stresses the idea of 'stewardship' (a concept emphasized by three of the union representatives), he sees this as essentially a proactive role in which clear leadership and direction is provided by a leader at crucial stages in a movement's development.

Reflecting upon his own leadership of the NUM he highlighted the changes he had witnessed, and in particular the development of a more direct and militant style of achieving change. 'A whole new way of life started after the dispute with the government in 1971. It seemed as if trade unions suddenly became aware of their position and their potential. Whereas in the 1960s, we in the Trade Union movement used to bemoan our inertia. I remember us complaining, "Well, we are really passive." "We observe only from the sidelines." "We do not affect politics very much." Now all that has changed!'

Part of that change he felt was a result of his own efforts and his own particular style of leadership. 'Remember that I had only been President for a matter of months. But I was very clear that we had to change things. I set out deliberately to restore the position of the miners' organization. To get back the respect we had lost. I had to generate public sympathy and also show to the world at large that we were realistic fellows. The miner, up to that time, had been portrayed as somebody that the country could easily do without. I had to clear that climate, and in order to do that, inevitably, I had to clash with the Government. And I clashed with them! Not only as the President of the NUM but also on a personal basis as well.

'I had to warn them. Because if as a union we had allowed things to happen in 1971 that could have been avoided, then I knew that the outcome would become the established pattern for British industrial life for the next decades. You could not conceive at that time of the Civil Service having a dispute with the Government or the Public Employees unions being involved in industrial action. To realize that that was unheard of in 70/71 shows how in one short decade the whole idea of trade unions and trade unionism has changed . . . and yes, I was at the beginning of all that change . . .

'Government attitudes change, and employers' attitudes change. Both have had to learn that whereas at one time they could take decisions which affected the lives of millions of people without having to consult them, without having someone to speak on their behalf, this has now changed. Years ago it would have been unheard of to consider talking and negotiating. Now it has become the pattern. A change which can only be good for both sides.'

For Arthur Scargill, the 'individual leader' concept *per se* is of limited importance. He holds that leaders are 'thrown up' by a wider based universal movement, and are only important in so far as they vocalize the concerns of that movement. They are, in essence and in reality, only the tip of a much more substantial ideological 'iceberg': 'I don't think individuals are the most important thing. I think that ideas and policies are what bring about change and that individuals come to the fore as a consequence of those policies, of that ideology, of that philosophy, whatever it may be.

'Individuals have obviously got ability and talent. To say otherwise would be nonsense. You cannot deny that somebody like Tony Benn has got ability. You cannot deny, for example in the National Coal Board, someone like Mike Ezra had got ability, but what happens is that people emerge in their given sphere as a consequence of certain other features.

'Now the power of the media is very important and one has got to recognize the impact of that medium on individuals, and on the way society and people generally regard individuals. So, therefore, I think individuals have got ability, have got talent, but the extent to which they emerge can, in many circumstances, be accepted as an accident rather than by design.'

In contrast, Sir Peter Parker disagrees by providing an 'illuminating' anecdote: 'I think the individual is enormously important, totally underrated. I used to take a bus early to work when I worked for Phillips. And I used to live in the Fulham Road in a third-floor cellar, and I used to catch a bus at 6 a.m. in the morning, go to Victoria, go out with a lot of jockeys who used to make their way to Epsom. I used to get off at Mitcham and I used to notice on the bus that if the bus conductor had personality and was "at it", the whole bus was kind of illuminated. Even on a wet Monday morning at 6 a.m. on this bus you'd get a terrific personality. I always used to think, "Marx never coped with him—this guy is alive and kicking", and I think you've somehow got to rehabilitate the individual in the scheme of things.'

## THE PROCESS OF CHANGE

Since all the people interviewed in this book were involved with change, we thought it might be revealing to find out what they felt about change itself in British society. Many felt that the process of change was not only complex, but in Britain, difficult to achieve. As Sir Michael Edwardes suggests, 'It is pretty difficult to bring about because there is more inertia in this country than almost any country I know'. Although the majority of our 'change makers' expressed similar sympathies, in one form or another, they were also optimistic about Britain's future in terms of the acceptance of social and technological change.

Sir Michael Edwardes felt that there were two primary influences for change in Britain. One is the outside pressures of the competitive economic environment, and the other is from individuals like himself, who for personal and other reasons, are 'change implementers'. 'Change comes about because of two factors broadly, I think. One is the interaction of other nations on us, i.e. who are exploiting our lack of competitiveness. I mean, it isn't government policy—the unemployment—it's a result of lack of competitiveness versus other countries. So I think that brings about change whether we like it or not. They simply stop buying our products. So that is change forced upon us by external forces. And then you've got people like me who bring about change with a view to trying to recoup the situation and to make us more competitive; and it is thought that the only way you do that is now by rushing out and employing a lot of people. You do it, in fact, by scaling down organizations to be lean, hungry and competitive, and to take on the Japanese and the Americans and the Germans. So you could say I am imposing change, as my detractors or those hostile to me would see it, or you could say that I am trying to reduce the imposed change which is being effected by people outside Britain who see us as a soft underbelly. I'm trying to control change, using change as the instrument to control it, whereas otherwise it is being forced willy-nilly upon us by other countries.'

Indeed, he goes on to suggest that one of the major problems of British industry is the lack of such entrepreneurial individuals. 'Well, if there are not enough individuals coming forward to take on the challenge of bringing about change in a nation that finds it difficult to accept change, then Britain will just go down the tube ... now we don't always throw up the individuals.'

Lord Weinstock agrees with Sir Michael Edwardes on the complexity of the change process. He feels that whether it is an individual on the shop floor or the Prime Minister, that ultimately it is the person who is at the forefront of any change in society. 'The whole process of history, of civilization, is really "How did we get from where we were to where we are?", which is really all about change, since we are not where we were, but there must have been change going on all the time—and change is going on all the time. So that change is not a modern phenomenon. Change is something that is organic and alive, and society, because it consists of people, is alive.

'What are we talking about—who are the people who form opinion? Now if you assume that popular opinion exerts enormous pressure and is even decisive in bringing about change, then we are talking about people who create influence, redirect popular opinion. Now it is a terrible mistake to think that those people are great national leaders necessarily; there is a fellow in the pub who is rather dominant in his little coterie and his views will be repeated by the chaps at the bench in the factory, over and over again. It goes all the way up to the shop steward. Wherever people gather together and there is someone who is more assertive than others, unless he is saying things that are entirely out of sympathy with what they feel, or some things that they feel, and they sharpen their perception of what society is like and what ought to be done about it. And mobilize even, although there is no particular focus at any particular moment, their support for some public figure who then comes forward and says "I have a policy for change", and that's it! Because at one sort of level—the present Prime Minister has been trying to bring about change on a major scale, a determined effort by the Prime Minister to lead the people to believe that the way they have become accustomed to carrying on is bad for them. That they need to change their attitude, to be more self-reliant, not to think that collective bargaining, extracting more wages, is going to improve their standard of living, because it will bring about their economic downfall, and may in due course take away their political freedom as well. And there is some evidence that although that perception of what she is saying may not be all that clear, she has altered people's way of thinking about what they should do and what they should have.'

Lord Weinstock also feels that one of the additional reasons why a person achieves success in changing society may be linked to the social movements of the time. 'So, the impressions of those individuals who have the style, the intelligence, the charisma and often the financial means to adopt leadership rôles expresses really quite popular movements going on in different strata of society, where resentments, ill-feeling, reflections of past sufferings, all become encapsulated in the perception of a man of power, or many men of power even, of influence, who say "We mustn't do that. We must change society in a certain way". Now, if those people actually get physical power and are able to do something about it, they will then try to give expression to the accumulation of ideas and ideals which they have amassed in the course of their experience. Those people will be of two sorts very roughly speaking. They may be of the Macmillan sort, who were influenced by their experience and saw suffering and wanted to do what you and I would call "good", and other people, who are simply egomaniacs, like Hitler, who wanted power and didn't care tuppence really.'

Sir Peter Parker, on the other hand, contends that the main resistance to change in Britain is man's innate desire for stability, the status quo, habit. He does suggest, however, that national habits sometimes provide the stability for change. 'Well I think that change takes place very reluctantly if humans are involved. I really think that change, unless you get a kind of energy in a person who is building the best mousetrap, then he will go on until he's built it, and he's commanded respect for it in the markets and so on. But if you're talking about change, it seems to me you have to decide changing what? I mean, what is it to be changed? We tend now to be worshipping a god called Change. I find myself saying "Strategy for Change" and everybody nods around the Board table. The real thing is changing from what to what, and therefore you've got to be seeing that change is a condition of a manager's life. You've got to get it into their heads—not too difficult to say it, but it's damned difficult for people to live it, because if we didn't have habits we'd go mad, if we had to decide everything every day. People tend to turn to habit, turn to routine, and of course you call it the Old Boy Network or whatever it is, it's there, and it's what keeps a show going.'

As we discussed earlier, Arthur Scargill feels that change can only occur by changing the society we live in, changing the mechanisms and abolishing the underlying class differences within society. 'Ever since I was 14 I wanted to change the world. If there's one thing that has happened now that I'm 43 years of age, it is that I'm more convinced than ever that I was right when I was 14! The only thing that's been brought home forcibly to me over the years is the correctness of my case. At the age of 15, I had only one ambition in life (a rather unusual ambition for a lad of 15), I wanted to be President of the National Union of Mineworkers—Yorkshire area. Something of course which I would never achieve. But it's interesting to think that that's what I wanted to be. I didn't want to be a manager of a mine, or a politician, or anything else. Although, funnily enough, I went through the developmental stages of being a leader member of the Young Communist League—I was the industrial organizer—I was involved at all levels in political work, and very active in what I would describe as pure politics as opposed to trade unionism. And it was only after recognition of where real power lay that I recognized that I would have to become involved in the trade union movement, if I was to change both the working conditions, the wages and fringe benefits for those I represented, but more importantly, if I was to change the society that brought those things into being and continue to preserve those class differences within society. And I realized that it was only by changing the mechanism that would eventually lead to change in society, that could possibly produce the end result.

'I think this change will continue in any society, because people, whatever system they live under, will want change inevitably. That doesn't mean change necessarily for the good. It could even mean change for the bad, as we saw in the 1930s in Germany. All sorts of factors again come into play, which produce a situation, out of which emerges a demogogue, out of which emerges a very unhealthy leadership, both in the singular and the plural sense, and that can be worrying.'

Arthur Scargill's predecessor, Lord Gormley, also sees social change in terms of struggle and conflict. But conflict in which a middle path can be seen and in which compromise is viewed in a positive light. He brought this flexibility into an area in which he was an acknowledged master. It became one of his main principles in what he would call the 'art' of negotiation.

'Oh, yes! Before I went into any negotiations, for example on wages (which is always the tip of an iceberg!) I would always have a very clear idea of what I could achieve, and where I ought to go. In negotiating you must never put yourself in an impossible position. That is what happens with a lot of negotiators. They put themselves on a kind of plank, and find that to retreat is very, very difficult. That is no way to negotiate! You have always got to have an escape clause.

'You cannot go into negotiations on the premise "it is this or ...". How easy it is to go around threatening. It is something that I try to avoid in other walks of life too. I would like the world to see that compromise is not a weak response, it is not giving in. Rather it is the true way to real change and progress. I have always firmly believed in that and I always will.

'If you want to bring about change and progress you have got to be in a position, and have the will, to compromise. If you have your position and the other person has his position then it seems sensible to begin to walk towards each other until you can find a midpoint where you can both agree that you have made progress. That, I believe, is what real negotiation is all about.'

Len Murray feels that there are a variety of change agents in society, various types of change processes: 'First of all there's the people who produce ideas. They may be a *scientist* working in a laboratory, looking for something and either finding it or making some description. Secondly, the *activator*, who's either putting it there, or sees the point of what he's doing or who may himself realize the gap in provision, which he commissions somebody to do. Thirdly, the *mediator*, who is subordinate to this driver, this Weinstock or whatever, and the third and fourth really come together, that's the *operator*, who gets the change into action, who designs the tools or who goes along with the workers and bargains with them, who finds the market—whatever the market is. It may be a market for a new motor car, or an idea to dissolve the Transport and General!'

Lord Longford sees the individual as the essential catalyst in the change process. Reviewing his own varied career, he told us 'I think he can operate on three distinct levels of action or involvement, each one calling for a range of different skills and abilities.

'The first is at the individual level. You probably know that a lot of people write to me on a personal level about issues and problems. That together with my prison visiting is how I try to change things on a one-to-one level. You can operate in that way. Or you may start up a movement or organization which involves others of a like mind. I started up the New Bridge for ex-prisoners, and the Youth Centre just around the corner in that way. Or, if you have a position of power or influence in our society you may use that. So I would make speeches in the House of Lords, or on the media or wherever, to try to get the law or current practice changed.

'But all of these different levels of action depend entirely upon the individual who instigates action; and they are all aimed at the same end, bringing about change.

'I have been fortunate as I have been able to operate on all these three levels, the individual, the organizational and the state.'

It seems, however, that most of our 'change makers' feel that the individual is still the most important factor. Len Murray sums this up succinctly: 'The individual is much more the operator—the man or woman who as the result of either a decision by some representative body, or because he or she is following an idea of his own, goes and changes something.' This approach to change in society is very close to Ottaway's idea that there are change implementers, change generators, and change adapters. That is to say, there are people who directly initiate change, while others implement it or adapt somebody else's ideas for change. On balance, though, each person we interviewed accepted the need for change and felt reasonably comfortable in the role of bringing about change. They also recognized the complexity of the change process and as Lord Longford aptly sums it up: 'If you are talking of people who bring about change, it is a strange and in the last resort an unanalysable equation.'

## CONCLUSION

In their recent book *CEO: Corporate Leadership in Action*, Harry Levinson and Stuart Rosenthal emphasize that change is created by individuals: 'If organizations are to satisfy human purposes, then the leader must not only have a cause but must also create a structure that both supports the development of the bond to the corporation and becomes an instrument for its continuity'. The majority of 'change makers' interviewed in this book would support this contention; that is, that the individual is at the forefront of the change process. In addition, they suggest it takes 'special people' to change organizations or society, individuals who possess what Lord Weinstock succinctly terms 'style, intelligence and charisma'. Many also felt that these 'special people' are 'natural or born leaders', who have acquired these skills during the course of life's experiences. In contrast, some feel that change is not only a product of 'the times and circumstance', but also that individuals are only the 'stewards' of change. Their existence is situationally determined and their role is to change the underlying ills of society, for instance, as Arthur Scargill suggested, 'abolishing the underlying class differences within society'. They all agreed, however, that change is a difficult, if not impossible process, because of 'man's innate desire for stability' as Sir Peter Parker emphasized earlier.

# CHAPTER SEVEN

# COMMUNICATIONS, RELATIONSHIPS AND DECISION MAKING

*'Getting results through people is a skill that cannot be learned in the classroom.'*

J. Paul Getty

*'Nothing is more central to an organisation's effectiveness than its ability to transmit accurate, relevant, understandable information among its members. All the advantages of organisations—economy of scale, financial and technical resources, diverse talents, and contacts—are of no practical value if the organisation's members are unaware of what other members require of them and why. Nevertheless, despite its overwhelming and acknowledged importance, the process of communication is frequently misunderstood and mismanaged.'*

Saul Gellerman

## COMMUNICATING: BREAKING THE BARRIERS

'One can lack any of the qualities of an organizer—with one exception—and still be effective and successful. That exception is the art of communication. It does not matter what you know about anything if you cannot communicate to your people. In that event

83

you are not even a failure. You're just not there.' These words of Saul Alinsky aptly sum up the importance of communication in the change process. Without exception, all of the 'change makers' interviewed saw themselves as communicators. Some of the members of our group believed they had been blessed with a natural ability in this area. Others admitted that they had had to work hard to learn and develop these skills. All held communication skills to be of the utmost importance if they were to function effectively in their role.

Sir Peter Parker, when talking about his time with British Rail, singles out this communicative ability as being of particular importance to him in achieving success. 'One of my greatest strengths is that I *can* communicate. It is an absolutely essential skill in my work as everyone must be clear as to my aims and intentions ... If you aim to change a massive organization like this one, then you have to get involved in communicating personally to every level. British Rail was so big, so ancient, so vast and so set in its ways that it was like trying to change the Grenadier Guards! Involvement and communication is the only way.

'I spend two days out of my office a week, have done from the start, meeting as many people as I can on the system. In my early two years I used to speak to eight or nine meetings a day—video stuff, get it around, talk to the chaps, let them ask you anything, anything, but be real to them. Stop and talk to as many characters as you can wherever you are, on the system, break the reporting lines, break the hierarchies, break the systems that breed bureaucracy.'

Sir Michael Edwardes, who during his time at British Leyland developed his own brand of direct communication with his employees to a fine art (often bypassing the established union mechanism), writes 'A key part of a successful manager's role is to communicate—first and foremost to his workforce, to explain and to motivate—but he should also be prepared to take his arguments and judgements to a wider audience, if circumstances warrant ... Industry has to work very hard at improving the communication skills of its managers.'

He told us that the clear communication of aims and intentions is central to positive management: 'That's the only way for me.

Telling people the facts, which is something that people aren't good at in this country. Leaders in this country don't stand up and tell people the facts. That's what I've been doing, the average chap on the shopfloor understands what I'm trying to do ...'

Lord Gormley has felt that one of the major problems with British industry is the fact that top management in many companies have never fully appreciated the importance of developing closer working relationships with workers, and openly communicating. 'I don't go along with the shouts and the screams you get sometimes from the CBI that the country's facing ruin because trade unionists are acting irresponsibly. I think at the moment the country's facing ruin because of the weakness of many management structures in the early days, where they went along glibly thinking they were in a position to just please their bloody selves and run their own industries, without the need to encourage the workers to be seen as part of it. I think it was that lack of communication which has caused half the problems they're facing today, and it's difficult to get some of these top managers that have been there for a long time to change their attitudes. Funnily enough, you get, I don't know what happens, some people get promoted to management from the ranks, and overnight there's a sudden change in their whole manner. I don't know why, I can never understand this at all.

'If you intend to do a management job, you must tell the people who you're going to manage, how you intend to do it! And you've got to tell them "If you don't think this is the best approach, then tell me, and let's discuss it thoroughly, in the interest of the firm we work for, because without the firm being a success (I'm talking now about a manufacturing firm), then there's no success for anybody".'

Arthur Scargill feels that it is not only communication itself that is important, but also the *style* of doing it. Reviewing formative influences and his present leadership skills he highlighted two key figures who had both in different ways stressed the crucial importance of communication. The first, 'the greatest orator I have ever heard', stressed technique, and Scargill has tried to emulate his powerful delivery ever since. 'The way I perform on a public platform, and I use the word perform in its literal sense, can stir that audience into an ecstatic reception, or it can leave them with polite applause, or simply with an acceptance of the speech, or whatever. It depends on my skills of communication, how the delivery is made. These skills are essential to a leader.'

His second mentor brought home to him the power of mass communications in bringing about change. 'He taught me the power of the media and that you had to communicate *en masse* whenever possible. That is why if I am invited to write an article for a newspaper I usually write it. Because, warts and all, it gives me the opportunity to say something, where the alternative would be to say nothing. The media is crucial to someone like me, and you need the skills to use it effectively.'

Clive Jenkins makes a similar point when he talked of the challenge and rewards of the mass-media. 'I do a lot of television now, that is all part of my business, pushing ideas off, and what a marvellous way to push ideas off! Mmm . . . just think of all those millions of people!

'Really it's teaching and preaching. It all goes back to that. It all goes back to the chapel. It's the same simple devices. Before the cameras start, or just before you go to the rostrum at a conference, you take three very, very deep breaths. You fill those couple of cubic inches at the bottom of your lungs that never get filled. So once you start, you start with a lot of extra oxygen in your system; it's simple things like that. Never twitch or look shifty. Lift your head up. Be clear and speak in sentences. Never start by saying, "Well, you know, kind of, sort of," and you will find people who do that can get over their message.

'Utilizing the media is a crucial tool, especially television. You get more letters from radio than television, but it is a marvellous way of talking to people. You see trade union officials at the turn of the century—if he did a mass meeting every day of his working life—would he have reached a million people? A million and a half? But with television I find that even on a minority rating programme you are always talking to at least 800,000 people!'

Clare Mulholland also feels that communicating 'without abrasion' is an essential requirement. 'I think my strength is that I have quite a good analytical mind, and I can express myself, and

I can usually communicate with people in a way that is not abrasive and so on.'

Len Murray feels that his career has taken him away from the face-to-face communication which he obviously values: 'I don't suddenly see myself bereft of any personality, but the thing I miss most is the face-to-face stuff, is the direct personal service stuff you get if you are a steward in a factory. Mine are very remote. Yes, people do come to me if they've got problems or I go to them if I've got problems. They've got more problems if I go to them than if they come to me!'

## TEAM WORK

Looking back over his time at British Leyland, Sir Michael Edwardes pinpoints increased worker participation and productivity as two of his major achievements. He attributes both to effective teamwork. 'There are ... two areas in the minefield of employee relations where much progress has been made in BL. Both are the results of great teamwork between the staff experts in the employee relations field and the line managers, with encouragement from the union.

'The first is in employee involvement, which requires line managers to lead, to appear among the men on the shop floor, to communicate with them, to keep them in the picture, and to treat them with the respect they feel and deserve. Only then will there be mutual respect. This has required a change of attitude on the part of the managers.

'The other major advance at BL is the increase in productivity which flowed partly from the new spirit, and which was made possible by new investment.'

As well as openly communicating their own views to employees, many of the change agents have felt that it is crucial to develop a team work approach. Mary Quant's husband, Alexander Plunkett-Greene, feels that the success of the Mary Quant organization is largely due to his wife's ability to develop a cohesive and interdependent team of designers and business people. 'Mary is surrounded by experts of this and that who all are on her side as it were, which is a terribly valuable thing for her, I think, because it means that she can get on with the thing she is best at. She has got a natural ability and she is also a very good politician, getting what she wants and so on, but she is surrounded on her side by people who are helping to do more or less the same thing. A lot of creative designers neglect surrounding themselves with a back-up team, which Mary has not done, and I think this is one of the reasons why she is more successful than other designers of perhaps equal talent.'

Mary Quant herself stresses the importance of team work: 'I know that an idea becoming a reality excites me. It has many of the problems of the film business in that it needs quite a large arena of people, of experts, to be got together to make it final, *as a team*. Each thing has to be right or there is no point and it is quite difficult to get that whole arena together, and all those people enthusiastic and believing in whatever we are going to make.

'The end product is good only if the team is good and that depends upon having a good relationship with every member in it. There are so many things that have to be got right all the way along. So you need to listen and be open to what people say; they know what they are talking about and they are often right.

'I don't see myself as a boss. I try to involve people, and I try to persuade. However, I know that I do have one great failing as the leader of the team. It is when I get very enthusiastic and I can't put something across quick enough to the others. I probably expect too much, I expect them to get something immediately when I have been stewing over it for quite a long time. Then I get impatient, impatient and very rude!'

Jeremy Isaacs also feels that team work and joint decision making are essential components of effective television. His *World at War* series was the product of such a team. 'What I've tried to do with most of the television I've been responsible for making myself, is to say something simple and direct and moving and important, if I could. In television, you can't do it as a dictator, because television is very much a team business, and I go on about wanting to take the decisions and have the responsibility, and be the boss, but the fact is I've always enjoyed working with other people, encouraging other people, bringing the best out of other people. It's not a lonely thing, where you're totally on your own as a writer is, it is an industrial product (if you like), and I have to work with other people to make it work.'

Such team work must involve an open door policy by individuals in senior positions. Lord Weinstock attempts to provide his employees with open access: 'As you can see here, there are two doors, and if you weren't sitting here, those two doors would be open with people going in and out of here all day long. No one feels obliged to agree with me about anything, and they don't agree with me all that much!'

In addition, and probably most important of all, is the fact that communication of any sort must involve a certain amount of listening. John Harvey-Jones feels that 'true success' depends on equal parts of listening and speaking. 'I know what I think is important for communication, and I believe communication is equal parts listening and speaking, or communicating. So it's building bridges and understanding, and understanding other people's points of view, and the reasons behind things that I consider to be communication. I have to say that a hell of a lot of successful people don't actually succeed. A lot of successful people I know are bloody awful listeners.'

## RELATIONSHIPS

Some of the individuals interviewed saw themselves not only as communicators, but as people who made 'psychological contact' with the people in their organizations. They felt that one of the most important characteristics in the communication process was opening up themselves as a person. Sir Peter Parker highlights the importance of the 'real relationship'. 'You talk about motivating managers, that's okay, but motivating managers means you're winding them up in some way. Actually the way you draw people is by making their relationship they have with you real, and that can't be faked. I mean, you can have a girl keep the cards of your top colleagues, so she knows when it's their birthday, but they know when it's mechanical and when it's really true. I think that whatever my weaknesses were, they would know my intention, they would know where I mean to be. I can communicate.'

John Harvey-Jones laid great emphasis, for successful management, upon the importance of 'a developed psychological awareness', an awareness of the interpersonal processes at work in the everyday situation.

'I know I have got these "process skills", I can lead groups of people to work as teams. I know I have got some abilities in those situations. Also I have got what I think of as "process imagination"; an ability to follow through at an interpersonal level what I think are the likely stages of a situation. That is very frequently described in this country as a "political imagination". I don't see it as political imagination at all but rather a form of process analysis.'

Even in his day-to-day operations John Harvey-Jones felt that this awareness of the subtleties of personal interaction is essential for the successful executive. 'For example, even at a very practical level, I have often found, as a "process observation", that when I am chairing meetings people inevitably call me John. But if at some stage somebody will say "Chairman" then I know to be on my guard. I know that is the stage where I have lost hold of the meeting. I know that is the stage at which I am in conflict, or I am not in tune or something, my antennae are out and hopefully I can respond appropriately ... It is a skill which is absolutely essential in my point of view if, as a manager leading a group of people, you are going to make anything happen, anywhere.'

Lord Weinstock feels that not only does he have to be a business entrepreneur, but also something of a psychologist, if he is to develop an appropriate management team. He feels that people at work should be treated not only with respect, but also with compassion. 'I have to see that resources are put to the best use in the interests of the people who are concerned with the company. Those people are the shareholders who own the company, those who work in the company (managers I regard as workers so we don't have to differentiate), and we have some common good, some collective shape, some common good to pursue. I mean, I won't do my shareholders any good if I have a depressed and discontented labour force. I won't do my workers any good if they are paid not enough money to induce them to make their best effort to work. I won't succeed if I have managers who do not treat the working people with the proper respect, which enables the working people to contribute constructively to the organization and the conduct of our industrial activity in the factories and so on.

'You don't treat everybody the same way. I mean, you know a fellow with a particular talent to do things is sensitive in certain respects. You must be careful that you do not say something that would upset him. There are some less susceptible people you can push harder, there are some people who are quick, there are some people who are slow, and you must deal with everybody. I also have to be a bit of a psychoanalyst or psychiatrist, or whatever word.

'Everybody is alone, we're all prisoners in this rib of bone and whatever—contact with people who you trust and have a feeling of love for, who rely on you and on whom you rely ... that is the great satisfaction.'

Jonathan Miller has managed successfully to combine his work relationships with his home life. He points out that most of his friends are actually work colleagues, or people connected with his work: 'Mainly people who live nearby or people who are artists, actors, and old friends from school, but on the whole my social circle has shrunk down very much indeed. In a way rather reassuringly because I like a quiet life. I don't like parties, I don't like dinners and I don't like entertaining. In fact I have a fairly simplified home life. I get most of my excitement in social life from the complicated hurly-burly of talking to these people. I love my colleagues and it is in the medium of the exchange of ideas and of mutual admiration of skills that I actually find the closest friendship.'

Mary Quant too spoke of the close relationships and lasting friendships that developed from working in what was often highly pressured situations. 'You must remember that ours is a season to season existence. From collection to collection. People work all-out and put everything into it and then there is a kind of lull until the next bout. It does mean that you have to be able to work intensely with all sorts of people in this way. And you can make some tremendous friends like that.

91

'Our clients are creative people too, but creative in a different way. Someone like Peter White from Dorma, who print and produce the domestic textiles, is a good example. We have worked together for over twelve years now and one develops a very exciting relationship over that time. Often I have worked with him right from the beginnings of my drawings. I have visited the factory, learned about their production problems and limitations, and shared in the solution of some of them. Peter has also become involved here and has made his contribution, adding to the drawings etc. So over the years we have developed a close two-way relationship and a very exciting and beneficial one at that.'

## MAKING DECISIONS

Another generalization that can be made about our 'change makers' style of operation is concerned with the degree of decisiveness in their managerial activities. Although this did not manifest itself in such a universal manner, it was still an attribute that distinguished many members of the group. 'Uncertainty,' Sir Michael Edwardes comments, 'kills business'.

Alistair Mant suggests that one of the characteristics (and a major failing) of the British manager is his inability to face up to and resolve (either for better or worse) conflict situations. 'The characteristic British approach is to *not* take decisions. A group of American businessmen will fight out the issue at length until the chairman says "Okay, we've talked enough—we'll do this!" The British pattern will be similar, except that the committee will somehow contrive to split 50/50, thus ensuring the postponement of the decision.' The reasons for this, he suggests, are cultural and historical. 'Britain has become predominantly a culture of Dependence—a drawn-in, reflective, unambitious place, revering the female gods of existence rather than the masculine gods of action.'

This is an observation which would meet with the full approval of Sir Michael Edwardes, who comments: 'There is more inertia in this country than in any country I know! ... the individual must be extremely frustrated at the decline he sees all around him before he decides to take on this mammoth national inertia.'

Perhaps this break from the strait-jacket of accepted norms is more easily made by individuals who see themselves as somewhat distant from society. Certainly, some of the innovators in our sample found that the fact that they came from outside the culture was a distinct advantage.

Sir Peter Parker was born in France and spent his childhood in China. Since most of his childhood was spent abroad, he was able to dissociate himself from the British class system, and he suggests 'it was a terrific advantage not to be carrying all that [social] clobber'. This meant that his decision making and industrial relations could be free from the constraints of a particular social class background and orientation.

It seems that these individuals are working within the structure of the system, but are not overawed or smothered by it in any way. As such they seem more prepared to take decisions and accept the full responsibility for their actions. As Lord Weinstock stressed: 'Success in industry needs the qualities of a man of action ... he needs common sense, conviction and courage.' And sometimes, he continues, action has to take precedence over protocol and tradition. 'Change makers', therefore, seem to adopt a management style which is essentially *proactive* rather than reactive, and they take on the role of leadership with some enthusiasm. As Lord Gormley clearly demonstrates: 'I always prided myself on being able and willing to do the job. That was something that was important. I was always acceptable in most companies because I could get along with, and work with, anybody. I think you've got to have these natural aptitudes if you're going to be a leader, and then I've a willingness to accept the responsibilities of leadership, because leadership is not just working because a committee has told you to do this and that and the other. To be a leader, you've got to lead. It's easy to lead men out, but you've got to have courage to lead them back!

'You've got to prove that you're a leader, you can't be a leader through a committee all the time. Some people will say "Well, I'll take it to my committee and get a decision"—that's leadership gone mad! That takes democracy too far all the time. Democracy is a maligned word—it depends where you start and finish. I think most of them, if they're successful leaders, will have to give you

93

that definition, because that's what leadership is all about, accepting responsibility.

'You have to make the decisions. Okay—you might lose some—but you win the majority. Another thing you've got to accept is you can't win them all! And don't take it to heart, and make it too much of an insult, just go round again! You've got to have that as well—to accept the fact that you can't always be right, although you don't want to lose too often! But leadership means just that—leading and accepting the responsibilities of leadership.'

Lord Weinstock echoes this view: 'You have to find out what is the objective. But when we have an agreement about the objective, if we had all the data, and if we are perfectly logical, we must all arrive at the same conclusion. But, since we don't have all the data, we never have all the data, there is always room for disagreement, not about the process, but either about the commencing premises, or about the objective. And we have to do what seems in the circumstance to be the most likely thing to be right when we *have* to make a decision. Sometimes we will decide *not* to make a decision, not to avoid the decision, just decide not to do anything today. And we look again next week or the week after or whenever, when we may have either more data or something will have occurred, or something else will have changed that was not foreseen. When we've made the decision, then we have to say "we may have been wrong", and we must continually review our decisions so if we see evidence that we were wrong we change them.

'One gets some feel of the results—some of the things we do are good, some of the things are not so good, and I regard all the not-so-goods as a personal failure. If I could have thought of the way of getting it right it would have been got right, and I failed to do it so I don't blame somebody else. If I have a bad manager, it's my fault for putting him there. One can't *do* everything, but one is *responsible* for everything.'

An ability to cut through superfluous detail to get to the heart of the matter is a good indication of the essence of this style. Mary Quant may see it as flair and inspiration: 'After all the discussion, I suddenly see it is simply the right thing to do, so my decisions don't seem risky, only right.'

Sir Michael Edwardes' personal assistant, when asked (by him) to comment upon his style of management, emphasized 'his ability to withdraw himself from the muddle and then to return and cut through all the difficulties. He is like a helicopter, one minute he is with you on the ground and in the middle of things, the next he is hovering above, looking at things from a clearer perspective. Suddenly he is back amongst you again, saying we must do this, this and this. It's very difficult to keep up with sometimes!'

Sir Peter Parker, when referring to his own style of management, highlighted the importance of *decisiveness* not only as an effective personal style but also in maintaining the dynamism of the executive group. He very much admired a colleague's 'remarkable cutting edge', and this was something he tried to emulate whenever possible. He described elements of this in his own boardroom performance, where he seemed to be able to see openings where others didn't: 'I use optimism like other people use a club. I go into a situation—actually sometimes stand outside the door—knowing the mood of the room and the meeting and then go in and just absolutely not accept it. Just ignore it and say, "This is marvellous news, isn't it?". And people say "What do you mean it's marvellous news?". And it's amazing how people can then look at it differently, like putting the lights up from this end rather than that end and the whole thing looks different.'

Indeed, prevented from exercising their own brand of decisiveness seems to lead to feelings of acute frustration, as Sir Michael Edwardes illustrates when describing the most difficult time of his career. 'My lowest point was when I didn't have the power and authority to do what I knew had to be done, and there are not many years in my life where that has applied! That was very, very frustrating, and frustration worries me. I wasn't frustrated at all at BL, despite the problems. I knew most of the decisions and solutions were in my hands or the hands of my team, even if we failed.'


**CONCLUSION**

The Spanish captain, Don Francisco Zarate, who was captured by Sir Francis Drake in 1579 commented on Drake's management style, 'He had nine or ten gentlemen with him, members of good families in England, who are members of his Council. On every occasion, however unimportant, he calls them together and listens to what they have to say before giving his orders—although, in fact, he pays no real attention to any one'. Alistair Mant suggests that British executives are similar to Drake in their leadership style, that is, that they engage in an 'autocratic management style disguised as participative management'. Although our study has found that people in top jobs are decisive, they are also self-revealing, open and communicative. Indeed, these skills seem to be the pillar-stones of their success. Almost all possessed a cluster of highly identifiable managerial skills. As significant individuals in their various spheres of influence, they shared traits that one would associate with a successful manager of people, contrary to the expected public image. They were 'open' about themselves, they believed in and evidenced 'open communication' and a 'close relationship' with their workforce and colleagues, they were decisive and believed in 'breaking the barrier', and above all they were committed to action underlined by a clearly identifiable philosophy or conviction.

# CHAPTER EIGHT

# ENERGY, PERSONAL STANDARDS, COMMITMENT AND CONVICTION

*'People are always blaming their circumstances for what they are. I don't believe in circumstances. The people who get on in this world are the people who get up and look for the circumstances they want, and if they can't find them, make them.'*

George Bernard Shaw

Alistair Mant, in his book on British managers, has tried to categorize senior and top executives into a number of different archetypes. He has talked about the 'Respectable Buccaneer', the swashbuckling Sir Francis Drake type who uses 'who he knows' and 'who he is' to achieve results. Or there is the 'Agent' type, who acts on behalf of others and takes no decisions himself. On the other hand, we may find the 'Scientific' manager, who tends to make decisions on what appears to be rational and appropriate data, but frequently ignores people problems. There is also a 'Quisling' type (either genuine or entrepreneurial), the individual who plays out the role of the 'pal' to his subordinates. Then there are the final two categories; the 'Technocrat' and the 'Constitutionalist', with the former concerned about technical aspects of the leadership role, and the latter believing fundamentally that psychological contacts between individuals or representatives of groups are essential for harmonious relationships at work.

After our interviews with the individuals in our group, we have been unable to fit most of them neatly into any one of these categories. We have found elements of all Mant's styles in each of them. What his categorizations ignore, however, are some basic fundamentals about the 'person' of the successful executive, for example, their level of energy, personal standards, and convictions. In this chapter we highlight some of the characteristics that we feel may be precursors to success.

## ENERGY

A high degree of drive and energy is held to be something which marks out the successful 'change maker' from his or her more mundane colleagues. It was singled out by our interviewees as an essential quality if the challenges and frustrations of effecting change are to be overcome. It was also a quality which they themselves seemed to possess to a considerable degree.

When asked what, if anything, opinion leaders might have in common, Sir Michael Edwardes said: 'All change agents have one thing in common, provided they are the right people for that role, they all have drive. That is the one thing they must have. They don't need a high intellect, but drive, yes, it's crucial.'

In a different context, Mary Quant is a symbol of this drive. She sees her creative ability as dependent upon 'some kind of adrenalin that jumps into action when opportunities are presented. Certain situations and challenges just switch it on!' She told us: 'I often work a 16-hour day, plus the travelling I have to do all over the world. I'm always working and living on a knife edge and I get very frustrated and impatient if things don't turn out as I want them to. We are all manic-depressives here! But I wouldn't change it for the world. It is tremendously exciting and it makes you feel very much alive!'

Sara Morrison acknowledges that, although opportunity and ability may be central to a successful career, motivation and energy are those extra ingredients which often prove crucial in practice. Reviewing her own skills she remarked, 'My real ability has been as a generalist. In part I think my success has depended upon knowing nearly enough about virtually anything that I need to. But also I had that little something extra which people found useful to have about. I think it was ... was that extra little bit of energy that made me laugh when most would have cried!'

Lord Longford, at an age when most would be happy in their retirement and having packed into his life enough experience to merit the *Seven Lives* title of his autobiography, was an example of this drive and energy. He exhibited such a high level of motivation that its extreme nature seemed to border on the obsessional. 'I've slowed up a bit, but I still work very hard. My work is my leisure, so it's not too bad, but I'm a seven day a week person. I usually get up at eight, have breakfast and read the papers. I spend half an hour on religious reading. Then some personal writing, my diary, and work on my current book. I come into the office [director of Sidgwick and Jackson] for a few hours in the morning. There is always a pile of letters to be answered or 'phone calls to be returned. These are usually "social work" type of problems. Then it's either the House of Lords, or committee meetings, or my social work interests in the afternoon until early evening. I've just started an enquiry into the aftercare of the mentally handicapped, so that is demanding a lot of time at the moment. I usually take work home with me and get to bed around midnight. I do work every day. You see, years ago I was told that if I was ever going to write anything whilst I was in politics I would have to do it at the weekend. I do not want to give the impression that I am as vigorous as I was. I am not. The truth is that I am in my late 70s and although I've always been a quick worker age has slowed me down.'

'Change makers', says Lord Longford, must have exceptionally high levels of energy. 'They have got to have drive and self-motivation. You feel every day has got to be filled. You must do something each day, achieve something. There is a feeling that you cannot waste a day.

'I've always had that feeling and this has become stronger with the growing years. I am in my late 70s now. I have not got so many years left and so much still to be done.

'I think you will find that these people cannot let many days go by without some sense of achievement.'

In a study published in *New Society*, Mary Whitehouse, another septuagenarian, possessed an impressively high level of energy. 'As a child I was absolutely full of energy, and I suppose I still am at 72. My team often complain that they can't keep pace. I have a very creative, quicksilver type of mind so I suppose it is difficult sometimes. Also I make things happen around me, so there is always something new to cope with.'

As we see, Lord Longford alludes to very full work schedules, which often spill over into 'unsocial hours', and this is typical of the group as a whole. Where part of a larger institution, they often seem at pains to prove that as a figurehead they are working as hard or harder than any of their subordinates. Arthur Scargill makes this point: 'I work extremely hard. I reckon I am the first in this office each morning and certainly I am the last out. I usually leave around 10 p.m., and that is every night. If I am to keep on top of my job, I have to.'

Describing his working day, Len Murray makes a similar comment: 'I get up at 6 a.m. and I'm into work before most people arrive ... the place starts to close down around 5 p.m. I stay on most nights and probably leave around 6.30–7.00 p.m. and then work at home for a few hours.'

This energy and drive is of particular importance when trying to change a large organization, as Sir Peter Parker illustrates. 'One of the physical bases for successful management is health. Like a politician really, you've got to have the energy of a bull. If you want to change a big organization like this you actually have personally to get immensely involved.'

The robustness of the person at the top must be of both a physical and mental type, as John Harvey-Jones suggests: 'The big difference between me and some other people in my company is I'm not interested in analysis—I'm interested in action, and making something happen. That's where I get my kicks.

'I think the second thing is robustness and the sheer ability to keep going. Energy—both mental and physical and actual sheer robustness. I don't think I have a spare lunchtime for the next four months!

'The principle on which I work is this. Because I try to divide my life up as I do (separating work from home), as soon as I leave home in the morning until the moment I get home at night I work all the time. Obviously I can't work while I drive myself to the station, but from the moment I get on the train I'm working. The moment I get off the train into my car until I reach the office here I work. I sort my mail; I have a dictation machine in the car so by the time I arrive here I have the tapes ready to hand over to my secretary ...

'My ideal would be that I ought to be able to do the job between 9 and 5. But I'm not good enough to do that. I find that I have a number of evening engagements and a lot of travelling, and I find I have to do a lot of representational stuff for the company. So the corollary of that is that you have got to try to use your time as efficiently as possible. And I mean efficiently. One of the great problems in Britain, and particularly in large organizations, is that people confuse activity with efficiency. I hope I don't fall into that trap ...

'All the same I work literally all the hours that God sends. I seldom go to bed before 1 or 2 in the morning, I always get up no matter where I am before ... I can manage on about four hours' sleep and I feel I must utilize every moment.

'I was in India for the first two weeks this year with my chief executive. His wife used to come in at one o'clock in the morning and make us go to bed. She would often come in and say, "It's all right for you John, you can stay up all night and still be all right in the morning!" and she would pack us off.'

This energetic approach can, of course, lead to fatigue, but the overwhelming drive and need to push themselves often prevents them from taking steps to minimize the stresses and strains of their job. Clive Jenkins comments: 'I would find it very difficult indeed to take a holiday. I'd switch off for a few days, but I'm the kind of person who always has to have a writing instrument and a piece of paper near at hand all the time—just to discharge the static of ideas. So I like a holiday now which is linked to work— I manage to get away from it a bit.

'Usually I can point back to a period of overwork. I'm one of nature's optimists. I'm a constructionalist—I think everything can be constructed, everything can be improved. So it's quite rare, and usually due to going over the edge of fatigue.'

## ACHIEVING PERSONAL STANDARDS

There are many possible explanations of what motivates people to reach the top in our society. They can be motivated by a need to control other people, a need to achieve success, a need for personal acceptance, a need for power to change an organization or society, or even a host of 'deep rooted' psychoanalytic factors. But many of the 'change makers' interviewed seemed to feel that their motivation came from 'within', that they were attempting to achieve some sort of personal standard.

John Harvey-Jones' early feelings of rejection by his father may have forced him on his own resources and standards: 'I often wondered why it has always been necessary for me to live up to very exacting personal standards, and it always has been necessary. And that sort of external approbation has not mattered to me. What's mattered to me is I've had to live up to standards which I set myself. What I have felt is a continuing need to prove myself, and I developed that partly because of my experiences in my prep school, partly because of that feeling of being abandoned. I certainly felt "dumped"—I didn't feel I belonged to anybody. I don't actually feel, I've never felt any impulsion for the success that is recognized by others. It's a curious thing, what drives me is *me*. I'm my own worst enemy at this.

'Again I have a characteristic—I am fairly introspective—and I'm terrified of fooling myself. So I'm very critical of my own analysis. What I believe I have done is I have always been interested in doing the job as well as I can. And doing the job as well as I can, I've never been particularly interested in fighting for promotion . . .'

Sara Morrison also views the battle as being with herself. 'If anyone had told me, when I was 18, that I would be doing this sort of job, I would never have believed them. But yet, looking back, I knew I wanted to do something really well ... At that age all I really wanted to do was to make certain that I rode my horses well, not just well but well enough to get to the Olympics and win a medal. I never believed in doing anything incompletely, that was always tremendously important to me. I suppose when I think about it, it was another form of the competitive spirit. But I never saw it as competing with anyone else, only trying to live up to one's own, often impossible standards.'

Self-satisfaction and achieving personal standards was also emphasized by Jeremy Isaacs. We can see once again the link between later motivation and early childhood experience: 'I think it was very much me I wanted to satisfy. I had felt alone, I had felt I had things to prove. I wasn't as strong as other boys, I wasn't as fast as other boys. I hated gym—I couldn't climb the wall bars—the usual stuff! I wanted to show that I really could do things.'

What was more interesting was the fact that this desire to achieve a personal standard of achievement was suggested more prominently by the female 'change makers'.

Prue Leith highlights what was found in a large-scale study of female executives in Britain, namely that women are frequently motivated to achieve self-set tasks and objectives without thinking about the consequences for their future career development. Women in top jobs seem to be ambitious in the sense of wanting to do things in the right way, to do the job to the best of their ability. Prue Leith reflects: 'People often say I'm ambitious. I don't think anybody does a thing without ambition, but I think ambition itself is a frightfully difficult thing to define. What makes you ambitious? I don't think I've ever been ambitious to earn a great amount of money ... I do think I've developed more ambition as I've gone along. At the beginning it was always the fun of it, that somebody would ask me to do something, and I'd think, "Gosh, I can do that, I'd really like to do that". And I certainly wanted a restaurant, that was ambition—foolhardy too, but I didn't know that! And I think I am more ambitious now, but I'm ambitious for doing things the best. I don't want a chain of restaurants, I don't want a second restaurant, I don't want any more—but I do want this to be the best one! My guys say I'm obsessed with the Michelin Star, but that's the trade accolade for really good cooking, and I'd knock a year off my life quite happily to get one! I really want one. And we spend quite a lot of time and effort making sure the food is good enough to justify it, so I suppose I'm ambitious in that, but it's because I'm ambitious to do the work that justifies the star. I don't just want the star, I want to be worthy of it.

'I think you get more satisfaction out of doings things well. If I write a chapter and I think it's good, then I'm happy, and it's no effort to work (proof-read it, alter it, edit or whatever), because I'm proud of it. I find being proud of things is very important to me. I suppose it's something to do with glory and vanity, because I like people to clap, and I need to feel that I deserve their clapping, not hollow clapping. I am ambitious, I suppose, but not for its own sake, I don't want to be wildly famous or rich, although I certainly wouldn't turn down a couple of million if you passed it this way, but I get pleasure out of the business doing well. There's a satisfaction over knowing that a business you own or run is doing well. I do believe (although it sounds pompous), that what you must do, is to do the job you're doing to the best of your ability.'

Clare Mulholland also illustrates the need to achieve self-satisfaction: 'I suppose basically I am an idealist, and I tend to think that people who are doing certain jobs are better at it than I would be, because only the best will do. One of the things with dawning maturity is that you realize most things are a compromise. A lot of people are only half-good, but for me that isn't enough. I have high standards that I constantly set myself, and so it may not be ambition, other than to do well. I certainly would want to do anything I took on well, and would be very frustrated and anxious if I didn't feel I had done so. I don't mean that you do everything wonderfully every day, but to see that gradually you learn and get better at certain things, and you build on the experiences that you've had. Again, I think I've been genuinely lucky in that although I've done different jobs, somehow or other it has given me a spread of experience that I can draw on, and every stage has given me something I can draw on. Even now, and I think that is the satisfaction—to feel that there has been a progression.'

Sara Morrison also emphasizes the importance of self-set

standards: 'I've been offered lots of interesting jobs ... all sorts of jobs which, when I was 18 if anyone had told me, I'd have had a fit. I just wouldn't have even thought about it. I don't know what I would have thought about, I would have wanted to do something—that was always true, but I just never believed in doing anything incompletely. That was always tremendously important to me, and I suppose when I think about it it was just another form of competitive spirit. I never saw it as competing with anybody else, I always just saw it as trying to do it to one's own satisfaction, which is virtually impossible.'

Elizabeth MacDonald echoes this sentiment. 'The other aspect which accounts for whatever success I might have enjoyed is the simple fact that everything I do I do to the best of my ability. I seem incapable of operating in any other way. I do not want to sound superior or self-satisfied because there are lots of things that I don't do at all! But when I do tackle something, whether it is getting a document together or gardening, I would do it absolutely to the best of my ability. That is how I view each task in my life. When I have been working I have not been looking simply for promotion. I have just been doing the job to *my* standards. I must say that I think that a lot of people tend to opt out far too easily. It might be better for their health and their private lives, perhaps it is. I don't know what category you would call that sort of person, but I certainly would not fit into it!'

## COMMITMENT AND CONVICTION

One of the most salient characteristics of many of the successful 'change makers' in this book is their commitment to their work and to life generally. They are men and women of principle, who are not frightened by confrontation or rejection or losing in the 'promotion stakes'.

John Harvey-Jones aptly illustrates his lack of fear of confrontation and its potential negative consequences: 'If I thought the job required doing something unpopular to my superiors, I've never hesitated in advocating it yet. I've always tried to advocate it and fight it in a sensitive and sensible way. I've not said "Look, the only thing you can do is this and by Christ I'm resigning if you don't do it", but I've fought and approached the problem in different ways. Gone on and on and on trying to make something happen, and that's been more important to me than my bosses saying to me "My God John, you're doing a great job".'

Our 'change makers' seem to be individuals who, at some stage in their career or personal development, feel that they must commit themselves to other people. They become more selfless, as Sir Peter Parker suggests: 'I do feel—I suppose I'm old-fashioned in the sense that I've got to be committed. And I feel that's very important, because if you come back to any sort of spiritual organization of oneself, the only valid position that you see in various cultures through history is that there is always the battle with your "selfhood", your selfish interests. The more you concern yourself with these, the more unhappy you become. Yet the reverse of that is to lose yourself, so that's selfish too, you could say. But in a way that part of the process is as much as you can manage in a lifetime, so you find causes that you feel make the best of you. And that's what I feel and I've always felt it.'

Some feel that their commitment to their job and their responsibilities to other people are at a minimal cost to themselves. They, in fact, are underestimating the risk-taking that their decisions and attitudes involve. It may be that some of them feel guilty about their senior position or their media exposure, and this guilt is reflected in their large commitment to the organization. Len Murray highlights this very issue: 'I joined the Communist Party and became active in the local trades council and so on, but I saw the trade union as being the way in which the things I wanted to see, and I use the word I in a rather arrogant sense, could best be achieved. Or the contribution that I could best make to achieving those things in terms of day-to-day democracy and building awareness and so on, rather than the participational sense.

'I miss the sense of achieving something, and then standing back and saying, "That's done, and I did it". Like when I cut my lawn! Here it's very difficult to evaluate, it's very difficult to put together a balance sheet—profit and loss and so on. You can see it over a period of time and you can stand back and see things that have happened and tendencies that have developed and how

106

you've managed to push something forward, or a challenge that you've accepted, or issued; particular things that you've done. Yes, a strike sorted out or an inter-union squabble dispatched—particular things like that, but those sort of incidents.

'This is a no-cost job. The danger is that you let other people carry the costs and pay the price. But I've always been very particular about that. Look through my diary and you'll find there are some weekends with a bloody great cross through them. That's the danger of it, but otherwise I'm almost fortunate—I really am. I get paid very well indeed for doing a job to which I'm totally committed, which gives me enormous satisfaction. I've got responsibility, I've got satisfaction.'

Others feel that they must be true to their own convictions. Lord Gormley's approach to leadership has been one in which he has followed his own convictions and has marched to the beat of his own internal drum. 'For my own self I've always tried to be Joe Gormley. I've always had my own style of leadership and that's why I sought and left the Labour Party Executive of my own accord. I left the TUC of my own accord—I said I must get out and not be stifled by any of this—I'll go and do my own thing—I'll do my job as leader of the miners.'

However, most of these successful managers have not allowed their job totally to dictate their lifestyle. Their internal convictions, their concern for their families, and their heightened ability to put the work and the home into context is one of the most cherished characteristics of these people. They certainly would not adhere to Studs Terkel's definition of work, 'Work is, by its very nature, about violence—to the spirit as well as to the body. It is about ulcers as well as accidents, about shouting matches as well as fistfights, about nervous breakdowns as well as kicking the dog around. It is, above all (or beneath all), about daily humiliations. To survive the day is triumph enough for the walking wounded among the great many of us.'

Jeremy Isaacs feels that if you are to achieve success, you must not only take knocks in life and be committed to a particular course of action, but you also must put your work into some more personal perspective. 'You have to have a capacity to think clearly, to take decisions, a great capacity for hard work, an ability to deal with people and relate to people, to listen to people and talk to people. It's very important to listen to people, and you have to find the energy to struggle towards perfection, the common sense to cut your losses and settle for what you can get, and you need an ability to be cheerful and take knocks and realize that tomorrow is another day. And in fact, very importantly, and this may sound an absurdity after what I've been saying, you have to understand that there are far more important things in life than work. I've had some terrible knocks in my family life. I lost a brother in a bomb accident (both my brother and his wife were killed by a bomb in Jerusalem), and I had to go and tell my parents that that had happened. And one knows all sorts of terrible things that happen to people who are close to one. And I think you have to give everything you've got to your work but the moment the work becomes the most important thing in life, you're on the wrong track somehow. I both think work *is* the most important thing in life, and I also think and *know* that it isn't that important!'

## SELF-DOUBT

One of the most revealing and unexpected characteristics to emerge from most of the interviews was the feeling we had that many of the men and women who are prominent in British business society are not the resolute and self-publicizing personalities we view on the television screen or read about in the papers. They are individuals who are more self-effacing and conscious of their fallibility. They are highly responsible people who are concerned about the power that they potentially possess and occasionally wield.

The most notable current example of this is Arthur Scargill, who is perceived by the general public and the media in a way that inaccurately reveals his true self. For example, he openly describes his feelings as he is about to approach a public platform: 'On a public platform I appear to be pretty arrogant, and there's a reason for it—I'm so nervous that to overcome my nerves I have to be ... well, I present my case in such a way that it appears that I'm absolutely arrogant, and in command of the situation, and

I've been on platforms when I haven't been able to hold my notes for nerves, but nobody knows that. I've appeared on television programmes and people have said "My God, you showed confidence, you told Robin ...", and I've been absolutely shaking. I once asked Harry Pollitt about this, by the way, and said "Will I ever be like you Harry? When will I ever get rid of this?" And he said, "If you ever get rid of it—you're finished. Whenever you're like this, it matters. And when things matter you'll do a great job. When they don't matter, that's the time to pack it in!" And I thought about that, and he's right you know. When I stand up and face my members, I'm nervous, and I'll tell you why—it bloody well matters.'

Arthur Scargill not only expresses considerable self-doubt, but also concern about the expectations of his members and their adulation of him: 'I think that someone with a cause will quite clearly emerge in a leadership position, whether it be at a very high level, or a low level. What worries me is the cult of the individual type of thing. And when I go around speaking and I find people are coming to standing ovations in wild ecstasy—it's very pleasant but at the same time worries me to a certain extent that you can get this kind of tremendous enthusiastic reception from people who believe you can literally "walk on water".'

Even John Harvey-Jones, the chairman of one of the largest UK companies, and by anybody's standards one of the most successful businessmen in Britain, expresses a certain lack of self-confidence. It may be that we in the general public and the employees in the organizations of the people we interviewed sense in them the compassion that must stem from a certain element of self-doubt. As the Chairman of ICI reflects: 'I've always sought the heat or the centre of the fire, and I've always felt the necessity to drive myself to do this. Having said that, I admire people very much like Arnold Weinstock for example, who have an unshakeable conviction in the rightness of what they do. I'm continuously plagued by self-doubt. I demonstrate, I think, a certain element of confidence, because I *have* to, because my chaps are entitled to it ... I mean, if they feel I don't know what the bloody hell I'm doing, well what chance have they got? But the whole time I'm questioning myself. Now, the curious thing is that when I've made up my mind, and I think I have the reputation of making up my mind very quickly and very easily, but I don't actually—I worry about problems. When a solution emerges, it emerges with a degree of clarity, which doesn't make me feel it's right, but makes me feel it's the only thing I can do. In a way the responsibility is thus resolved. I can still worry, but I've analysed all the various actions that one could take, and I know that this is the only one that I can take.'

Lord Gormley reflects on his time as President of the NUM: 'Of course I worry like hell, I'm worrying all the time, to see whether things are going right or not, and make sure that anything we're doing is not going to weaken our position, both from a trade union and a political point of view. I worry all the time, it would be stupid for me to say I don't worry, of course I do. But I don't like to let others see that they worry me—that's the difference, you see, you've got to carry it with you.'

The inordinate responsibilities of some of these senior people, whether in industry or in the trade union movement, can be a source of pressure. They are well aware of the expectations of others, in solving industrial problems or obtaining business or even solving the difficulties of the national economy. Len Murray, former General Secretary of the TUC, and Lord Weinstock, one of the top men in British industry, reflect on the pressures of expectations. As Len Murray comments: 'The danger with this sort of thing, this sort of job, is that you can begin to believe that you're entirely on your own about it—that it's *you*, and that when *you* speak, it's something that should be heard. Why have you come to see me? Not because I'm young, intelligent and handsome, but because I'm General Secretary of the TUC—I'm a representative of the TUC. And anything I can do, any influence I've got, any authority I've got outside, comes from *that* fact. But some people I've known have confused the two things and have thought they can solve the world's problems.'

John Harvey-Jones talked at some length about how throughout his career he had a continuing need to prove himself. 'What drives me is *me*. I am my own worst enemy.' Yet underlying all of his successes are those same nagging doubts suffered by several of the group.

'I always, always start on the assumption that I can't do it! That applies equally to work. I always believe that I cannot do a higher level of job. I know that I can do the job just ahead of me. But I have never believed that I can do the five or six jobs ahead of me.

'I suppose looking back that I have had a very quick career in ICI at least by ICI standards. I well remember explaining over and over again to my wife, that there was absolutely no way that a non-technical man like myself could possibly get to any substantive level in ICI. Then I remember when I was Sales Manager saying, "Well, you know, there is just no way that I could make it to an ICI Divisional Board." Then when I made it to the Divisional Board I explained to her that there was no way I could be a Deputy Chairman or even if I could just remotely be a Deputy Chairman, then there would be no way that I could be a Chairman of the Division. Right up to the time that I was chosen for this job I was still totally convinced that I would not get it.'

It is interesting to note that John Harvey-Jones previously mentioned Lord Weinstock as an example of a resolute, supremely confident manager, who has 'an unshakeable conviction in the rightness of what they do'. Lord Weinstock himself, however, admits: 'I have a fear of failure—I don't like to let anybody down. That's a thing that worries me—that I might make a bad job of something, or that somebody who was relying on me might find that that was unjustified.'

We have seen earlier how Jonathan Miller was greatly influenced by his father's success, and how he initially intended to follow a career in medicine, like his father. It is obvious that he still has lingering regrets about this: 'I sometimes think that the reason I work as hard as I do and have such a high rate of productivity as I do is partly because I feel it needs 25 or 30 items of theatrical work to make the balance for any one item of medical, scientific work not done. Although I know that I do serious, good work in the theatre, I can never convince myself that any work in the theatre is of any importance at all.

'I think I am very much influenced by my father who was, after all, a person who had achieved respectability and importance in his own field. On his death-bed, I can see him still in St George's

Hospital, rearing off his pillows, clutching his breast and saying "I'm a flop".'

Some find that the constant glare of publicity, and often adverse publicity, adds to their feelings of insecurity. Jonathan Miller, again, is concerned about this: 'I get written about, perhaps in a more systematically hostile way than others, possibly because I do more things. Very few people have had such a long series of lambastings in *Private Eye* as I have had, that's gone on and on and on. It bothered me when it first happened and then I gave up looking at the magazine, but one has always got 'friends' who tell you how badly you have just been written up.

'Now when that happens it also coincides with one's fantasy and self-estimation, which is that much worse. So that if one was sublimely confident of what one was doing then you could enter into a sort of arrogant indifference, but you don't because it often coincides with one's own anxieties.'

John Harvey-Jones emphasizes: 'This is a terrible thing to say, and it's not totally true, but I don't need to be loved. I don't like being disliked, but I can even put up with that. I can understand that I irritate a hell of a lot of people. An awful lot of people look down their noses when I hover around the headlines and so on. I appear on television and I give views on things, because I actually believe that the voice of industry has to be heard in this country, and I die a death before each one of them. I loathe it! And my family loathe it. Even the dog loathes it—he bites me when I get home! But you know, it's a part of the job, and the fact that one would actually prefer that nobody recognized you—I don't get a kick out of being recognized if I'm wandering around ... Who's interested in you, as you?'

## LIVING UP TO OTHER PEOPLE'S EXPECTATIONS

Not only do other people expect these 'change makers' to be able to solve problems, but they also anticipate that they are able to build the future. Lord Weinstock feels that he must do better for his employees to secure their jobs and standards of living. 'One is preoccupied by having to keep doing better. One gets on this treadmill, and if you don't do better, people will stop you. We don't try to do things right, we try always to do things better. All that impetus to do things better depends to some extent on the dominance people have. So one is left feeling one must do better, not because doing better means anything to me particularly, making more profit etc., it depends on how one makes the profit—it may not be constructive. There's the idea that one is in perpetual limelight and judgement by the public at large who I don't know, and who don't know me, but to my own work-people that is considerable pressure. They feel better if they think I'm okay on it. If not, they don't feel so good about it.'

Consideration of his employees' interests was also important to John Harvey-Jones. 'Well, the nature of me is that if I've got a problem, I've got to confront it. The ones that cause me most pain are "people problems". Business problems and so on, it's almost an act. Don't get me wrong, I'm involved, but if we lost XYZ order, that won't make me go bananas. In fact, even if I felt I'd crease, I feel it an absolute necessity to demonstrate that, you know, "So what?". No, I think the things that cause one most pain are people problems, and particularly in this kind of company, which has a terrific reputation, well-deserved, for caring about its people. One of the problems is that we haven't been successful enough to care about our people in the way I'd like to care about our people. I am driven by a great feeling of expectation of our people, and if there's a feeling that I've let them down, that really is what creases me. Now that feeling doesn't have to be expressed by mouth. That feeling is usually subjugated, but I'm very conscious that there's nobody who can carry the banner for the whole of this company except me. So, if I haven't done well enough in projecting us onto some external ground, I kick myself. I kick myself particularly if I feel I've taken a thing too easily or not taken enough trouble, or there was something I could have done which would have made it go better.'

## CONCLUSION

Levinson and Rosenthal, in their book on American Chief Executive Officers, suggest that 'leadership itself is a form of play', that is, that work can be a playground for successful managers. 'When one is in love with one's work, then the extraordinary hours are like play ... Despite its burdens, they [chief executives] enjoyed the work they were doing and made of it a kind of play.' It was certainly true in our study that many of those we interviewed spent long hours at work and possessed Herculean levels of energy. In contrast to their American counterparts, however, our group of British 'change makers' saw work as an opportunity to commit themselves, to achieve some personal standards. Work provided them with the foundation stones to achieve some individual goals, which could have some wider social or personal meaning.

It may be that the British, and perhaps European, senior managers, in contrast to their American counterparts, have a deeper responsibility and commitment to the organization and society that have allowed them the access to and exercise of power and influence. Is this an indication of a more highly developed 'social conscience' among the British senior managers and/or an indication of the American concern for individual acclaim and recognition?

# CHAPTER NINE

# WHAT IT TAKES
# TO REACH THE TOP

*'I hold strongly to this: that it is better to be impetuous than circumspect; because fortune is a woman and if she is to be submissive it is necessary to beat and coerce her. Experience shows that she is more often subdued by men who do this than by those who act coldly.'*

Niccolò Machiavelli

Our research has given us useful insights on leadership behaviour from a selection of men and women who have achieved success. To put our conclusions into context, we felt it would be helpful to provide a brief summary of some of the earlier studies on the characteristics of leadership.

Placing the individual within the process of change and the debate about his/her powers and necessary attributes has a long history. Plato described his 'philosopher king', a rare individual possessing those superior abilities as befits a 'man of gold'. In the *Republic*, he opens up the basic debate as to whether leaders are born or created, a debate which is still energetically carried on today.

The nature/nurture controversy, and its separation into two discrete and disparate approaches to leadership, crystallized in the late 18th and early 19th century. Then philosophers engaged in heated argument as to the relative importance of 'great men' as

115

individuals versus the situational context in which they operated. At one extreme there were those, like Nietzche in Germany, and William James and Emerson in the United States, who believed that the personal characteristics of individual leaders determined the course of history. And in England Carlyle proposed a similar theory. These individuals, Carlyle assumed, possess talents superior to their peers, which enables them to emerge and function as effective leaders. Emerson suggested, however, that whilst the role of leader was important in the development and direction of specific society, nevertheless, these 'great men' represented in one person the general 'will of society' as a whole.

Both Carlyle and Emerson, however, agreed that the 'leading men' of their day, as of any other period of time, possessed something in the way of special and unique talents which enabled them to achieve their position and, having achieved it, to work effectively within it.

Weber, writing at the end of the 19th century and presenting a sociological perspective, identified 'charismatic' leadership as *the* elemental form of authority. Unlike the 'traditional' and 'rational' bases of power, charismatic authority arose directly from the personality of the individual. 'Charisma ... refers to an *extraordinary* quality of a person, regardless of whether this quality is actual, alleged, or presumed ... the governed submit because of this belief in the extraordinary quality of the specific *person*. The legitimacy of charismatic rule thus rests upon the belief in magical powers, revelations and hero worship ... the source of these beliefs is the "proving" of the charismatic quality through miracles, through victories and other successes ...'

Opposed to the 'great man' approach were the environmentalists, such as Durkheim and Spencer, who asserted that it was the 'Zeitgeist' or situation rather than a specific individual which determined the course of change in society. These philosophers maintained that the leader was nothing more than an expression of the needs of his time. If one man did not emerge to fill this need, then another would step forward to do so. According to this school, man's power to change the situation was extremely limited, if not illusory. Great men were simply an expression of the needs of that period or situation.

Others would argue that, however made, the individual can rarely be the arbiter of events. Bismarck, who in the final analysis must be considered as having influenced enormously the social and political events of his time, remarked, 'The statesman can do nothing of himself. He can only lie in wait and listen until amid the march of events he can hear the footsteps of God. Then he leaps forward and grasps the hem of His garment. That is all he can do.'

The dichotomy between these two opposing approaches holds true for today's researchers and theory-builders. So much of the early work aimed at discovering the *traits* of the leaders is a logical development from the earlier philosophers' 'great man' theme. Likewise, the modern exponents of the environmentalist position are those sociologists and psychologists who have attempted to study the effects of *situational* factors upon leadership and entrepreneurial behaviour.

## THE SEARCH FOR COMMON TRAITS

Early research examining common traits followed closely the seminal work of Galton, who, in his book *Hereditary Genius* in 1869, demonstrated the linkages among persons of outstanding achievement in a variety of fields. Consequently, much of this earlier research focused upon isolating the physical, intellectual and personality traits that distinguished a leader from his followers.

Havelock Ellis in 1904 carried out the first empirical study of 'British men of genius' (in actual fact he used the term 'genius' as practically synonymous with 'eminence'). He emphasized the balanced personality of his subjects 'who showed very little psychosis, although minor nervous disorders and poor health in childhood were rather frequent'. Later, Godwin in 1915, in his classic book *The Executive and his Control of Men*, differentiated between 'thinkers' and 'doers'. In this study, he attempted to link physique directly to leadership. In particular, Godwin found that successful executives were taller and heavier than the people they controlled! Also his research indicated that those in executive positions, the so-called 'doers', were taller and heavier than those individuals he classified as 'thinkers'.

This categorization according to physical type reminds one of the Kretschmer-Sheldon schema of the relationship of physique to personality. By careful measurement of both physique and personality, they established clusters of traits which corresponded closely to specific physical types. Sheldon's work supports Godwin's in that larger and heavier physiques are more likely to be associated with extroversion, i.e. that such people tend to be 'doers' and executives rather than 'thinkers'.

By 1926, Cox found that the two most important characteristics of great leaders, intellectuals and artists were their 'persistence' and 'drive'.

In yet another early investigation, Tead in his 1935 book *The Art of Leadership*, reported that the traits of the 'effective leader' were 'nervous and physical energy, a sense of purpose and direction, enthusiasm, friendliness, integrity, technical mastery, decisiveness, intelligence, teaching skills and faith'. Barnard, in *The Function of the Executive* in 1948, stated that the significant traits that distinguished leaders from their followers were physique, technical skills, perception, knowledge, memory, imagination, determination, persistence, endurance and courage! Other writers and researchers identified characteristics such as adjustment, good appearance, need for achievement, assertiveness and fear of failure as being necessary leadership traits.

The trait approach came in for severe criticism in the 1940s as the list of 'essential' attributes grew to absurd lengths. This was largely because there was little discussion and agreement as to how the concept of leadership was being used by the various researchers. Fraser highlights this difficulty: 'It is simple with hindsight, to see how this profusion could have come about. As the number of studies increased, so did the range of tasks and situations, and it is unrealistic to expect the same set of people to be leaders right across the board ... Even the de Gaulles and Mao Tse-Tungs of this world are probably happy to pass the initiative to others should they find themselves in situations where limousines will not start or Cabinet Ministers faint.'

Since that time, and probably as a result of these criticisms, trait studies have been less ambitious in scope and consequently more reliable in their findings. Re-reviewing the situation in 1974, the eminent American psychologist Stogdill, in his *Handbook of Leadership*, is somewhat more encouraging. Whilst he recognizes that different situations will demand of the leader a specific set of skills and abilities, there seem to be some general characteristics that seem to be present in most effective leaders in most situations. He suggests that the effective leader can be seen as exhibiting 'a strong drive for responsibility and task completion, vigour and persistence in pursuit of goals, venturesomeness and originality in problem solving, drive to exercise initiative in social situations, self-confidence and sense of personal identity, willingness to accept consequences of decision and action, readiness to absorb interpersonal stress, willingness to tolerate frustration and delay, ability to influence other persons' behaviour, and capacity to structure social interaction systems to the purpose at hand.'

In a similar vein, Shaw, writing two years later, summarized this literature by pointing to a number of generalizations. On average, effective leaders will score higher on 'measures of ability—such as intelligence, amount of relevant knowledge and verbal ability; of sociability—such as social participation, co-operativeness and popularity; and of motivation—such as initiative and persistence.'

## BEING THE RIGHT PERSON, IN THE RIGHT PLACE, AT THE RIGHT TIME

However central psychological characteristics are in ensuring the eventual success and effectiveness of the leader, they constitute only one element in what is a complex equation. Although the range of skills, abilities, and underlying drive are important in themselves, for us to attempt to account for the success of the individual in these terms alone would be shortsighted in the extreme.

Situational factors, although we do not examine them in detail here, are obviously extremely crucial and we must acknowledge them, if only in passing. Allport, the renowned American psychologist, concerned as he was with the importance of the individual, realized that this was only one element of a range of forces and that any worthwhile theoretical account must encompass them all. He advances a model which suggests that there are three factors which determine personality development. In the first instance he sees the course of individual growth as depending upon the *chance factors* of inheritance and environment. Then there are the *opportunistic factors* such as the opportunity to learn certain skills, or to take up a particular role or position. Finally, there is the factor of *propriate striving*. This is a natural force within the individual which moves him towards maturity or 'creativity' and which expresses itself in the course of the life the individual leads in order to satisfy that drive.

In our study, we only examined the final factor of the three and we did not explore the situational elements in any depth. Certainly the subjects themselves saw circumstances as being of particular importance in their personal development. Important that is in determining the direction in which they would find success rather than in determining success itself, which they saw very definitely as resulting from their own efforts and abilities. Mant highlighted these situational factors, when, along with 'the capacity for serious work' and 'a personal pressure', he suggests that the success of an executive depends on a large element of luck, 'the chance conjunction of man in a state of readiness with a particular situation'.

Although luck is usually ruled out, as we might expect from a group of individuals who 'make things happen around them', *timing* is seen as a different matter entirely. It was singled out by a number of the group as being a very important element in their success. Timing seems to be based on an ability to overview a complex situation, to see the opportunities and pitfalls, to match available resources to the demands of the situation and finally to formulate a clear plan which is then acted upon. Mary Quant says of this, 'Success has depended largely on an equation of abilities, timing and opportunity. My timing has always proved to be lucky. I seem to have done exactly the right thing at the right time ... I've always had a lot of that sort of luck ... But really it isn't luck at all. Certainly in my case what people have called luck was really hard work and good timing!'

Sir Peter Parker reinforces Mary Quant's viewpoint when he says: 'Colleagues would probably see me as lucky, but I don't believe in luck. Timing is all. What I seem to be able to do is make the appropriate decision at the right time and that is everything.'

Arthur Scargill sees successful leadership as a combination of weighted elements, which can in certain circumstances come together in a sort of synergistic equation. 'The leader emerges as a result of a combination of forces. First, there is his own ability and talent and expertise. Secondly, there are the extra leadership qualities required, and finally, there has to be the opportunity ... each element has a weight and if they are not all present to a certain degree then the leader is unsuccessful or ineffective. I have emerged as a leader simply because a combination of all these elements came together at the right time.'

## THE SEVEN ELEMENTS OF SUCCESS

Most people have a 'theory based on practice' idea of what makes success. Len Murray, for example, when asked about leadership qualities and success, suggested: 'First, they've got to have a sort of crosswordy kind of mind. They've got to see connections between things, they've got to put things together—a jigsawy kind of mind—they've got to see relationships between things. Secondly, they've got to be able to express rather complicated things in intelligible language—whatever the language may be in the group within which they are operating. Third, they've got to have a certain passion, they've got to really want to make something happen. And fourth, they've got to be prepared to get a bloody nose, or to make a howling mistake and pick themselves up and carry on, and explore alternative ways of securing the change they want to see, or abandoning that idea anyway as not being practical, or acceptable. They've got to be persistent, and as part of this acceptability thing they've got to see and understand how people will react to it, the articulation and presentation, i.e. judging how they will react and then making a presentation that will obtain the results they want. Finally, as part of the persistence thing, they've got to realize that introducing change where a lot of people are concerned can often be a tedious, and painful process.'

John Harvey-Jones would broadly agree with Len Murray's observations. He told us, 'I have looked with the same sort of introspection as you are now doing at the common factors in successful people, and I can only actually see three. I do believe it has a lot to do with your early upbringing, which perpetuates this achievement orientation. The second as I have already told you is energy, mental and physical ... the ability to keep going ... And the third is communication, the rare ability to get over your ideas to all levels and all groups and at the same time to be open and receptive.'

From our interviews, discussions and many hours of listening to tapes and reading transcripts, we have been able to identify seven elements common to our group of 'change makers'. Some of these you may see in Len Murray's 'seat of the pants' theory, others may reflect your own 'common sense' views, and still others may provide a new insight into the characteristics, attributes and experiences of people in top jobs.

## 1. *Childhood*

It is obvious from earlier chapters that early childhood experiences and influences are partly responsibile for what Mant terms 'the entrepreneurial personality'. One can see the direct link, for example, in Sir Peter Parker's childhood and his ultimate success in business. 'My own "watershed" experience was, of course, the family, and the family being battered by economics, and therefore feeling, "I've got to master that, master the economics. Your independence depends on that." I remember my father used to send me to the public library to watch the Chinese dollar going down from 1s 2¼d to 3¼d. I used to go down and look at it, so I've always felt that you've got to master that [economic security]. You've got to understand how *that* cookie crumbles!'

Most were able to highlight a 'watershed' experience, often occurring in their early years, which seemed to have a profound impact upon them at the time and was seen often as a turning point in their own development. Arthur Scargill commented: 'I think, if anything, the first thing that impressed me or my young mind sufficiently to compel me to think about national and world events as a youngster, and left an indelible imprint, was reading in a newspaper a rather innocuous article describing the death, through starvation, of about a million Chinese people. This was just around the end of the war period in 1945, and I couldn't understand how, in the same paper reading of modern technology producing so much grain in the United States, that they were burning it in railway engines in Canada and the Mid-West. Now it seemed to me to be inconceivable that any society that called itself civilized could on the one hand produce an abundance of food and destroy it, and on the other hand report glibly that up to a million people had died of starvation. I thought there must be something rather corrupt and rotten about that! And I suppose *that* as much as anything influenced me as a youngster to begin to think actively about doing something.'

Childhood was recalled almost without exception in terms of deprivation and loss. Deprivation not in simple economic terms of grinding poverty, although we have seen that several of the group came from very humble beginnings, but rather in a psychological sense. A loss of, or a separation from, key 'significant others' at a crucial stage of their emotional development.

At one extreme, Lord Weinstock's and Len Murray's early formative years were parentless, both experiencing the traumas of an 'orphanic existence'. In their case responsibility for their early upbringing rested with close and 'not so close' relatives. In the case of John Harvey-Jones, the loss was just as severe and the 'orphanic existence' just as real when, at the age of six, his parents left him in the care of an English prep school.

Others in the group were raised in 'one parent family' situations. Here, by necessity, mother became the dominant caring figure. The father, where present, was often rarely seen and conceived as a rather unreal, distant figure, often idealized in the subject's eyes.

The key theme that emerges from these experiences was one of insecurity and loss. In the dependency of their childhood, they suffered because they were victims of circumstances beyond their control. Parents appeared and disappeared, even 'stability of place' was lost through family mobility or war-time evacuation. The resultant emotional state was often one of anger: anger at the pain that was caused, and anger at their own helplessness in the situation.

Freudian psychologists will tell us that threats to the psyche, particularly those experienced in early years, are often countered by defensive, 'compensatory' action. In the case of our group, these early negative experiences have led to a need to regain control of their environment, a process which in itself brings that psychological security which they lacked in childhood.

## 2. *The loner/independence*

As we have seen, most of the group shared a background in which they experienced some form of psychological deprivation and insecurity.

Although these childhood experiences were seen as painful and traumatic, most considered that they had emerged from the experience with added strengths of self-reliance and 'survivability'. Strengths which would serve them well in their future careers.

As young children they had often found themselves isolated or alone. This meant that even at a tender age they had had to rely much more upon their own resources than children from more 'normal' backgrounds. In addition, many originated from 'minority' groups or had been born or raised outside of our mainstream society. And whilst Sir Peter Parker might see the lack of 'all that clobber' to be advantageous in later life, it did mean that developmentally they were likely to have suffered the double disadvantage of childhood insecurity and a marginal identity!

Perhaps then we should not be surprised that one of the key attributes to emerge again and again from the whole group was the idea of being 'a loner'. Childhood and adolescence was marked by few close friends. Perhaps even at this stage their earlier experiences produced an ambivalence towards trust and dependency which resulted in an enforced isolation and independence.

Activities were often of a solitary nature; most told us that from an early age they were avid readers and rarely engaged in shared childhood activities. Even in adolescence they only invested in a few well-tried relationships. We found that these were patterns that often persisted into their later years.

Again, this quality of independence and self-sufficiency can be explained as a defensive reaction against painful experiences. Loners do not get close and therefore are safeguarded from both loss and rejection. This self-containment has continued into adult life, where it is recognized by most as a major personality trait and a desirable one at that. The end product is a person who psychologically is well defended and secure in their own self-sufficiency. Several individuals hinted that they saw themselves as part of, and yet in some ways apart from, the society in which they operated. As we have remarked elsewhere, 'To overstate the case, it seems that while society might have need of them, they do not feel they need society to the same degree'.

### 3. *Motivation and drive*

Energy and drive were crucial to the success of these individuals. Sir Michael Edwardes' observation, that 'All change agents have one thing in common ... they all have drive', was a sentiment echoed in one form or another by the majority of the group. Certainly, it was an attribute all seemed to possess in abundance. Energy, for life in general and work in particular, came over in the face-to-face situation and was reflected in a seemingly hectic work style. Even at an age when most would be happy in their retirement, Lord Longford, the most senior of the group, was almost obsessional in his level of motivation. His 'typical day' would do justice to a person half of his age! As Mary Quant remarked, 'Change agents need to be adrenalin addicts'.

The functions of the leader are to direct and to enthuse. There seems no doubt that their *own* individual level of motivation had a spin-off effect, and acted as an inspiration and a model to their working colleagues. These people did enthuse and mobilize people, largely because of their own energies.

When close colleagues of Sir Michael Edwardes were questioned about the advantages and disadvantages of his leadership style, they thought that simply keeping up with him was one of the greatest challenges! We were told, 'One thing about working with him—it's certainly not dull! Everyone else is stimulated because of the atmosphere'.

Sir Michael Edwardes himself has no doubt of the effectiveness of the highly motivated manager. He firmly holds that 'everything flows from the top' and that the leader must provide the positive model for others to emulate. As he further suggests in his auto-biography, '... my view [is] that business is about leadership; it requires understanding, courage, single mindedness, drive and an ability to persuade and lead others.'

We have seen earlier that frustration with the perceived status quo, frustration often bordering on aggression, is one of the mainsprings which drive these people. The motivation to achieve and make a mark upon their environment, 'to control a naughty world', is another facet of a basic need to control their own destiny, and may explain their need to make things happen. As we have seen elsewhere, the only time Sir Michael Edwardes could remember being bored was when he had no control over events and little challenge to respond to.

Of his later years at Chloride, colleagues thought that if anything he seemed almost bored with his continuing saga of success. Perhaps they were picking up the feeling of 'not being stretched enough'and the beginnings of a need to move on to seek out riskier or more challenging environments where the odds would be greater and where success, were it to be won, would smell even sweeter.

Sir Peter Parker also had little patience with resting on his laurels. Talking of his own achievements and questioned about the security success might bring, he replied with force and feeling. 'I don't know security. I don't want to know it. In fact, I don't believe that "security" is a view of life tenable to me!'

Indeed, the only stressful areas that Sir Peter Parker would acknowledge were the feelings of limited achievements and the passing of time. 'Growing old. I don't like that at all! The sense that you can do so little for the big things you care about ... The feeling that I haven't done enough, not anything like enough ... I wish I had nine lives. My God, I wish I had nine lives!'

In Freudian terms we see a group of individuals who possess extremely high 'ego-ideals'. This is that part of the conscience which directs our 'should' behaviour. It is, according to Freud, formed through our early experiences as a dependent child, and is particularly influenced by relationships with those 'significant others', usually parents, who nurture us at this stage of our development.

The ego-ideal is an ideal state towards which the ego is continuously striving. Freud suggests it is largely unconscious and provides direction to our 'life forces'. It is literally an ideal, and like most ideals it can often be unrealistic and, therefore, in the last analysis, unattainable. Loss of 'significant others' during the early formative years, and the deprivation of role models, is likely to result in an extremely high and unrealistic ego-ideal in later life.

Unfortunately for the individual there is always likely to be a gap between the ego or self-image and the ego-ideal. The greater the gap, the greater the energy invested in pursuing these demands of conscience. If there is a shortfall, then the angrier one becomes with oneself the harder one pushes to close the gap.

All of the leaders in this book talked of standards which suggested high ego-ideals. Often they referred to a constant striving for an end product which they never did fully achieve, 'a pursuit of ever-receding goals'.

Levinson and Rosenthal's analogy with respect to American CEOs applied to our group of 'change makers': 'These leaders were like trout swimming against swift currents. They couldn't stop. They stayed alive in a metaphorical sense by encountering and enduring in the cold, harsh, forceful environment in which they lived. Indeed, they sought the advancing currents; they sought change. Theirs was an upstream orientation ... these men could be characterized by a sense of restless dissatisfaction.'

#### 4. *Belief system*

Since the individuals in our group are often actually concerned with the process of disequilibrium, we found that most need, and have found, a secure platform or source of personal stability.

This they have achieved through allegiance to, or identification with, some 'mission' or cause, which in itself, is greater than themselves, but in which they play an important and often defensive role. This well worked out belief system gives them an inner security and confidence, and provides both purpose and direction to their endeavours.

When we talk of the 'well-integrated personality' we are talking of the individual who has clearly worked out his or her ideas on the 'meaning of life'. Someone who in psychological terms has a 'cognitive map' which provides clear and meaningful direction in what is often a confusing situation. It helps the individual to bring order from disorder. Through it they are able to make sense of the past, act effectively in the present, and direct their actions in the future.

Though most members of our 'change makers' considered themselves essentially as individualistic operators, they also saw their actions as part of a much wider philosophical perspective. Without exception they have well-developed and clearly articulated value and belief systems in which their own actions are precisely located.

In practice, it does not seem to matter what the exact nature of the belief system is. Rather it is the function it plays in providing not only direction and purpose, but also justification and support when they are under pressure. For Lord Weinstock it was rooted in a mixture of the Protestant ethic and the use of logic; for Sir Peter Parker it was a guiding belief in the social functions of business and a pursuit of a mixed economy approach; for Arthur Scargill the cause involved his commitment to socialism and the inevitable conflict of class; and for Len Murray, Lord Longford and Richard Ingrams, it was a particular branch of established Christianity which provided an ultimate meaning to their actions.

A clearly articulated system of belief means that the desired end results are clear and that the 'boundaries' of appropriate action have been well defined.

Clarity, both of vision and of purpose, is the end result. Psychic energy, skills and abilities are not wasted in questioning the mission, but directed and focused upon achieving the desired goals. Being part of a greater cause or mission not only sets the wider context for individual action, it also provides security and support in adversity, motivating the individual in times of difficulty and setbacks.

5. *Early responsibility*

Many of our group were highly motivated to succeed even from childhood. Some had even identified their desired careers at an early age. We have seen that Sir Michael Edwardes started his entrepreneurial activities in his late teens, Mary Quant her fashion designing at an even earlier age and Arthur Scargill his commitment to political activities as soon as he had left school. Others took some time to find their eventual vocation, often exploring, like Jonathan Miller and Sir Peter Parker, other professions or totally different areas of activity.

Most shared, however, one common attribute. They had experienced a relatively high degree of responsibility at an early stage in their career. This, we believe, gave them a unique advantage over their peers. It provided them with an opportunity, in what was often a relatively safe environment, to develop their embryonic skills. Managerial and leadership ability, not to mention motivation and 'sticking power'—we should remember that not all of the group achieved instant success—were tested out in real situations. They were able to find, in what Sir Michael Edwardes would term 'the space', an opportunity in which to flex their muscles.

This 'managerial moratorium' was a time in which responsibility could be explored, failures could be made, and retrieved, and mistakes tolerated and turned into constructive learning experiences.

In addition, these early years were often marked by a degree of success. Many of the group could be identified as 'high fliers' even in their youth. They showed a well-developed drive for achievement; a fast growing range of skills and abilities; an ability to capitalize on opportunities that came their way; and the evidence of proven performance and successful experience. These qualities often resulted in a degree of formal recognition. Some were 'scouted' by larger organizations (Edwardes, Parker, Weinstock), whilst others launched into entrepreneurial activities (Quant, Ingrams, Miller, Leith), often creating their own organization in the process. The end result was an early flying start on the road to their eventual success.

6. *Charisma and leadership approach*

All the individuals in our group, as leaders or senior executives of influential organizations, were powerful people. Their power came not only from their position at the head of the organization, but also from their *leadership style* and their own *personal charisma*.

Charisma is a somewhat mystical concept, yet in practice it is well recognized in managerial circles. Perhaps it suffers from being 'too well known and too little understood'. In this instance, what we mean by *charisma* is the ability to inspire others. It was a quality possessed by many of the leaders we interviewed.

Although charisma is a quality which is difficult to analyse, it seemed from our observations to be dependent upon a cluster of key elements. Certainly the high level of motivation is important. As we have noted elsewhere, the enthusiasm and drive that these people brought to their task is striking. It is easy to see how this can create a dynamic atmosphere which rubs off on subordinates and sets standards for the organization as a whole.

Successful organizations achieve their aims through purposeful behaviour. Although some goals may be blurred and certain market forces unpredictable, most success is based upon thrust and direction. Organizations without thrust are moribund; without direction, ineffective. Charismatic leadership provides both drive and direction.

Research suggests that ego strengths and a well-integrated personality are marks of the charismatic figure. We have noted earlier that a leader was likely to possess self-confidence, clarity of purpose, and the security of a well-established belief system. This combination can provide a powerful image and model to all within the organization.

Charisma means visibility. Inspiration to be effective must be public. Many of the individuals within the group stressed the importance of 'leadership image', both to subordinates and to society at large.

As might be expected, the heads of the largest commercial concerns, Edwardes, Harvey-Jones, Parker and Weinstock, were particularly conscious of their 'figure-head' role. They saw this aspect of their managerial function as enabling individuals within a large organization to achieve a clearer corporate identity.

### 7. *People skills: communications, decision making and establishing relationships*

Communication skills were seen to be central to their success. At the macro level most were well versed in utilizing the media. Those with a 'figure-head' role were well aware of the importance of developing a 'platform presence'. A presence which would inspire, and would engender confidence in the public figure who was at the head of the organization. Many prided themselves in their ability to cope with what Sir Peter Parker saw as the 'thespian role' of the manager.

Mant suggests that there is a universal mythology about the work of people in top positions. Challenging the conventional wisdom, he suggests that 'real management work is characterised by variety, discontinuity and brevity. Decision-making, one of the main planks of the rational/scientific management idea, tends to be done through the "seat of the pants" or "off the top of the head", or in some other place, but rarely in an orderly fashion'. This may be perfectly true, but our study indicates that those who achieve senior positions in society are able to deal with uncertainty and change. In fact, top positions seem to attract not the logical, rational technical operator, but rather as Sir Michael Edwardes was described by a leading industrial psychologist, 'a dynamic, organised man who flourished within chaos'.

Each person in our group seemed to possess high levels of ability in communicating, establishing relationships, facilitating the activities of others, acting as catalysts and, most importantly, encouraging organizational synergy. We noted that the skills high-lighted by our group of successful people were not those you would find as central features of the curriculum of most estab-lished business schools, where economics, financial planning, mar-keting and production management reign supreme! Even the oc-casional course of personnel management rarely ever touches the importance of communications, team management and awareness of interpersonal behaviour. These very characteristics, though, seem to be the touchstones of success for our group of successful people. We should note the failure of our educational system to convey the importance of these skills. Our group were forced to learn these skills through bitter experience. They were, however, fortunate enough early in their career to be in a position which allowed them to learn the lessons of 'people management'.

## CONCLUSION: THE 'SUCCESS FACTOR'

What, besides their success, marks the members of our group as being in some way different from their peers? Can we account for this extra ingredient, this 'success factor' which makes them exceptional?

We can see a number of general patterns emerging, admittedly at times somewhat hazy and not all-inclusive, but themes which do occur with startling regularity even in our small group of 17 individuals.

• *Early childhood experience.* We believe that early childhood experience is a significant element, particularly in the formation of their basic attitudes and their perception of themselves vis-a-vis the world. Childhood, for many of our group, was in the psychological sense a period of insecurity and loss. This led to a subsequent drive and need to control their own future.

• *Loner.* In many cases, these childhood experiences developed self-reliance and 'survivability' in the members of our group. The element of being 'a loner' emerged again and again.

• *Motivation and drive.* A further element in the success of the group was motivation and drive. This stems as much from their need to regain and exercise control of their own destiny, as from their pursuit of financial or organizational goals.

• *Supraordinate belief system.* Each member of the group had a well-developed value and belief system. While these varied from individual to individual, this key element gave each a clarity of vision and purpose.

• *Early responsibility.* An important additional ingredient was that each of our group had taken on a high degree of responsibility at an early age. This allowed them to develop the managerial and executive skills they would need later on in their careers.

• *Charismatic leadership*. Leadership style and personal charisma were common to all the members of the group. This element of charismatic leadership provides both drive and direction to the organization.

• *Communicator*. The ability to communicate was the final element that each of the successful people possessed, particularly the ability to allow themselves to be open and honest about their feelings and attitudes.

The overall picture, therefore, that emerged from our study and was contrary to the popular myth, was of a group of highly motivated individuals, often driven by anger and frustration with the status quo. Many had a deprived background of some kind, and many subscribe to what we labelled a 'supraordinate belief system'—a belief in something greater than themselves, whether Christianity, socialism or the work ethic.

George Bernard Shaw described these individuals perfectly in his book *Mrs Warren's Profession*, 'People are always blaming their circumstances for what they are. I don't believe in circumstances. The people who get on in this world are the people who get up and look for the circumstances they want, and if they can't find them, make them.' These are the people that Britain needs in the future, by the hundreds and thousands, if it is to prosper, and to remain a humane industrialized society.

# REFERENCES

3 'the game character is happiest': Michael Maccoby, *The Gamesman* (London: Secker and Warburg, 1977).

3 'so badgered by a sense of internal emptiness'. Alistair Mant, *The Rise and Fall of the British Manager* (London: Pan, 1977).

3 'In the office in which I work': Joseph Heller, *Something Happened* (New York; Ballantine Books, 1975).

3 'Self actualising people': AH Maslow, *Toward a Psychology of Being* (New York: Van Nostrand, 1968).

4 'The childhood shows the man': John Milton, *Paradise Regained*.

11 'In an earlier study': CL Cooper and L Thompson *Public Faces, Private Lives* (London: Fontana, 1984).

12 'In his autobiography': Michael Edwardes *Back from the Brink* (London: Collins, 1983).

13 'He had more influence': Arthur Scargill, *The Sunday Times*, 10 January 1982.

25 'A man like me cannot live without': Sigmund Freud, a letter to Wilhelm Fliess, 1895.

29 'It is important for everyone to believe': Alistair Mant, *The Rise and Fall of the British Manager* (London: Pan 1977).

34 'I feel that one has got to be strong': Petula Clark in CL Cooper and L Thompson, *Public Faces, Private Lives* (London: Fontana, 1984).

38 'When I went to Cambridge': Enoch Powell, in P Hingley and CL Cooper, 'The Loners at the Top'. *New Society*, September 1983.

42 'Herman Hesse in his book': Herman Hesse, *Demian* (St Albans: Panther, 1969).

42  'The whole work of man': Fyodor Dostoevsky, *Letters from the Underworld and other Tales* (London: Dent, 1913).

43  'It (work) is about a search': Studs Terkel, *Working* (New York: Avon Books, 1974).

43  'Alistair Mant, in his book': Alistair Mant, *The Rise and Fall of the British Manager* (London: Pan, 1977).

49  'the concept of creating space': Michael Edwardes, *Back from the Brink* (London: Collins, 1983).

55  'Even when the path is nominally open': Virginia Woolf, *Women and Wanting* (London: Women's Press, 1979).

55  'According to the International Labour Office': *Year Book of Labour Statistics* (Geneva: I.L.0., 1979).

61  'Toto, I have a feeling': Frank L Baum, *Wizard of Oz* (London: Dent, 1965).

61  'there are only three times': St Augustine, *Confessions*.

62  'Mental health is not so much': A Kornhauser, *Mental Health of the Industrial Worker* (New York: J. Wiley, 1965).

62  'At the very top': Joseph Heller, *Something Happened* (New York: Ballantine Books, 1975).

71  'work at least gives him': Sigmund Freud, *Civilisation and Its Discontents* (London: Hogarth Press, 1963).

72  'It should be borne in mind': Niccolo Machiavelli, *The Prince* (Harmondsworth: Penguin, 1961).

72  'If I have reached any conclusion': Michael Edwardes, *Back from the Brink* (London: Collins, 1983).

81  'This approach to change in society': RN Ottaway and CL Cooper, 'Moving Towards a Taxonomy of Change Agents'. *Management Education and Development*, Vol. 7, No. 3, 1976.

82  'If organizations are to satisfy': H Levinson and S Rosenthal, *CEO: Corporate Leadership in Action* (New York: Basic Books, 1984).

83  'Nothing is more central': Saul Gellerman, *The Management of Human Resources* (New York: Holt, Rinehart & Winston, 1976).

83 'One can lack any of the qualities': Saul Alinsky, *Rules for Radicals* (New York: Random House, 1971).

84 'A key part of a successful manager's role': Michael Edwardes, *Back from the Brink* (London: Collins, 1983).

92 'Uncertainty kills business': Michael Edwardes, *Back from the Brink* (London: Collins, 1983).

92 'The characteristic British Approach': Alistair Mant, *The Rise and Fall of the British Manager* (London: Pan, 1977).

96 'autocratic management style': Alistair Mant, *The Rise and Fall of the British Manager* (London: Pan, 1977).

97 'People are always': George Bernard Shaw, *Mrs Warren's Profession*

97 'Alistair Mant, in his book': Alistair Mant, *The Rise and Fall of the British Manager* (London: Pan, 1977).

100 'As a child I was absolutely full of energy': P Hingley and CL Cooper, 'The Loners at the Top': *New Society*, September 1983.

103 'Prue Leith highlights what': M Davidson and CL Cooper, *Stress and the Woman Manager* (Oxford: Blackwell, 1983).

107 'Work is, by its very nature, about violence': Studs Terkel, *Working* (New York: Avon Books, 1974).

114 'When one is in love with one's work': H Levinson and S Rosenthal, *CEO: Corporate Leadership in Action* (New York: Basic Books, 1984).

115 'I hold strongly to this': Niccolò Machiavelli, *The Prince* (Harmondsworth: Penguin, 1961).

115 'And Plato, in the *Republic*': (New York: Basic Books, 1968).

116 'Weber, writing at the end of the nineteenth century': M Weber, *The Protestant Ethic and the Spirit of Capitalism* (London: Allen & Unwin, 1930).

116 'Charisma ... refers to': HH Gerth and CW Mills (Eds) *From Max Weber* (London: Routledge and Kegan Paul, 1948).

117 'Early research examining common traits': R Galton, *Hereditary Genius* (London: MacMillan, 1869).

# References

117 'who showed very little psychosis': Havelock Ellis, *A Study of British Genius* (London: Hurst and Blackett, 1904).

118 'This categorization according to physical type': E Kretschmer, *Physique and Character* (London: Routledge and Kegan Paul, 1925).

118 'By 1926, Cox found that': CM Cox, *The Early Mental Traits of Three Hundred Geniuses* (California: Stanford University Press, 1926).

118 'nervous and physical energy': O Tead, *The Art of Leadership* (New York: McGraw-Hill, 1935).

118 'Barnard, in *The Function of the Executive*': CJ Barnard *The Function of the Executive* (Boston: Harvard University Press, 1948).

119 'a strong drive for responsibility': RM Stogdill, *Handbook of Leadership* (New York: Free Press, 1974).

119 'measures of ability': M E Shaw, *Group Dynamics* (New York: McGraw Hill, 1976).

119 'Allport, the renowned American psychologist': GW Allport, *Pattern and Growth in Personality* (Boston: Harvard University Press, 1961).

120 'the chance conjunction of man': Alistair Mant, *The Rise and Fall of the British Manager* (London: Pan, 1977).

125 'To overstate the case': P Hingley and CL Cooper, 'The Loners at the Top, *New Society*, September 1983.

127 'These leaders were like trout': H Levinson and S Rosenthal, *CEO: Corporate Leadership in Action* (New York: Basic Books, 1984).

131 'real management work is characterised': Alistair Mant, *The Rise and Fall of the British Manager* (London: Pan, 1977).

# INDEX

# INDEX